For Grandma T.

about the author

Berit Thorkelson is a freelance writer who grew up in the Valley of the Jolly Green Giant. She has written or cowritten books, including *Only in Minnesota,* as well as lots of magazine and newspaper articles about the North Star State and beyond. Berit lives in an 1890 farmhouse in Saint Paul that she is renovating with her husband, an Iowan.

You Know You're In Series

you know you're in
minnesota when...

101 quintessential places, people, events, customs, lingo, and eats of the north star state

Berit Thorkelson

INSIDERS' GUIDE®

GUILFORD, CONNECTICUT
AN IMPRINT OF THE GLOBE PEQUOT PRESS

INSIDERS' GUIDE ®

Copyright © 2006 Morris Book Publishing, LLC

Text design by Linda R. Loiewski
Illustrations by Sue Mattero

Library of Congress Cataloging-in-Publication Data
Thorkelson, Berit, 1971-
   You know you're in Minnesota when—:101 quintessential places, people, events,
customs, lingo, and eats of the North Star State / Berit Thorkelson.
        p. cm. — (You know you're in series)
  Includes index.
  ISBN 0-7627-3895-2
  1. Minnesota—Miscellanea. 2. Minnesota—Description and travel—Miscellanea. I. Title.
II. Series.
  F606.6.T48 2006
  977.6'053—dc22

                                 2005025935

Manufactured in the United States of America
First Edition/First Printing

to the reader

You know those stories about people who kind-of-sort-of knew each other in grade school, then met again at a reunion decades later and realized they were always meant to be? That's like me and Minnesota. I grew up here happily enough but left at age 18, figuring those were enough years spent in any one place. After bouncing among different states and countries for a decade, I landed back on Gopher soil. Accidentally. Just for a while.

Within one week a friend from another state marveled at how I'd slipped back into the long Os and As of my native tongue. "That sure didn't take long," she laughed. Which, of course, made me a bit defensive—she *was* laughing at me—until I realized that the Minnesota accent wasn't the only thing that felt comfortably familiar here. The lakes, the loons, the Twin Cities, the windshield scraping, the long good-byes, the hot dish, the hockey, the north-woods. To my surprise, I really didn't feel like leaving. It was good to be home.

Well, of course the state I'd spent the better part of my life in felt comfortable, and of course time and space allowed me to appreciate what I'd formerly taken for granted. But there was more to it than obvious state symbols. There's a vibe, for lack of a better term, that I find difficult to describe, but it has something to do with how Minnesota Wild hockey games are perpetually sold out, how the arts blossom and are historically well supported, how people run outside on the snowiest of days, how Minnesota Public Radio produces so many National Public Radio programs, and how the United Way consistently names Minnesota the most caring state for its "strong climate of charity and civic engagement." Things like that, which create, or are created from, some independent brand of self-esteem wrapped in collective pride and bolstered by Minnesota Nice (see page 52). Recently, a frequent visitor from another state put it to me like this: "In Minnesota, in the cities and the small towns, it feels like everyone is leaning toward each other."

It was good to hear this from someone who does not live here since I do wonder what someone less involved in the state, someone *not* able recite the state's counties in reverse alphabetical order, perceives. By the time this man had told me his Leaning Theory, I'd spent many months entrenched in the process of writing this selective Minnesota encyclopedia of sorts. It was fun narrowing down the list. There were the obvious must-includes, such as the ones I mentioned earlier—the accent, the loons, the lakes, and so on. But with the help of many other Minnesota natives I call my friends and family, these core icons quickly spiraled out into many more items than I could possibly address. What kind of book about Minnesota wouldn't mention the Mayo Clinic? Or the North Shore? Or Bluff Country, for that matter?

Then there's *uff da*. And Garrison Keillor. Walleye. Lutefisk. And, oh my God, of course the Vikings. Boot hockey. Lutherans. The Guthrie. 3M. Snow days. With only 101 slots, clearly some tough decisions had to be made.

Decisions were made, lines were drawn, and the result is the book you are now holding. (All the aforementioned made the cut, by the way.) Thanks to Minnesota lifers Christopher, Romelle, Brian, Dad, Chuck, and Dave for giving it a studied once-over, and to Clint, my boyfriend living in his native Iowa at the start of this project and my husband living in Minnesota at its end. The book is meant for both the categories he now straddles: state know-it-all and state newbie. I love listening to Clint's observations and questions as he eases into the former. My favorite part is when we're returning from a trip somewhere, no matter how lovely, and our shoulders relax, the mood evens once we're within the state's border, and we know we're headed for the Wabasha Street Bridge or the High Bridge, with the Mississippi below us and Saint Paul huddled before us, and we're struck silent by the feeling that we are lucky. And that it's very good to be home.

3M, the company behind such ubiquitous products as Scotch tape, Post-It Notes, and those combo yellow sponge/green scouring pads, was founded by five Minnesotans in 1902 as Minnesota Mining and Manufacturing. That second *M* never really panned out. The idea was to mine corundum in Two Harbors, on Lake Superior's North Shore, and use it as the sandlike element in sandpaper. The mine yielded a different mineral that proved an unacceptable substitute. Its weight also collapsed the second floor of the company's two-story plant. Not a great start for Minnesota Mining and Manufacturing.

The company forged on, sticking with the sandpaper idea but buying the needed mineral instead of mining it themselves. Saint Paul businessman Lucius Pond Ordway lent financial aid, and the company hired William L. McKnight, who started as assistant bookkeeper and eventually became 3M's president and guiding force. By 1916 the company had moved to Saint Paul, was completely out of debt, and had even paid its first dividend.

McKnight encouraged customer feedback and employee input. This philosophy, along with 3M's research labs, has led to more than 55,000 products and operations in more than 60 countries. Beyond masking, recording, and cellophane tapes and abrasives of all kinds, 3M is behind Scotch-

3M:

The name stands for Minnesota Mining and Manufacturing, the international corporation founded and based in Minnesota that gave the world, among other things, the Post-It Note.

guard Fabric Protector, diaper-fastening tabs, reflective materials on highway signs, synthetic stadium grass, Thinsulate, and metered-dose asthma inhalers. And get this: When Neil Armstrong took that first step on the moon, it was actually his 3M-made synthetic spaceboot soles that made contact. Bet the company's founders never dreamt that up when they were faced with a collapsed plant and a bunch of subpar sandpaper.

For a look at this multibillion-dollar worldwide company, check out the modest 3M/Dwan Sandpaper Museum—yes, sandpaper museum—in Two Harbors, the town that saw the company's humble beginnings. For more information, call (218) 834–4898.

you know you're in
minnesota when...
...long Os and As are longer

First off, our state name: It's not "Min-eh-SEW-ta." It's "Min-uh-SŌH-duh." You can even hold the "SŌH" briefly, for effect. *O* and *A* sounds are long here, though less dramatically so for city dwellers or perhaps new and returning residents.

A good rule of thumb: The lower the population density, the stronger the long *O* and long *A*. Same thing happens the farther north you go. And if you're headed in that direction, another crucial word whose pronunciation you should be aware of is *lake*. This is pronounced "lāāāk" here. Really hit that *A*.

New users of the Minnesota dialect should practice these two words until they come naturally before building up to more complex sentences, such as, "Hey. Let's take the boat out on the lake." Once that rolls off the tongue as, "Hāāāy. Let's tāāāk the bōōōt ōōōt on the lāāāk," you could pass for a local. If that's your goal, you really should practice the usage of other words and phrases, including *then*, *now,* and *you betcha.* And dress the part—wear a sweatshirt.

A and O:

Sounds that Minnesotans often pronounce long and drawn out.

Bōōōt
Lāāāk

you know you're in
minnesota when...
...you have lunch and buy bait in the same building

It's easy to fish in Minnesota. Lakes are everywhere, and so are bait shops. These places that sell minnows, night crawlers, leeches, and other things fish want to eat are often combined with other sorts of businesses, commonly gas stations. Even in the Twin Cities metro area, you can buy bait alongside fountain drinks and fuel.

With the need so great, other types of establishments have incorporated bait into their standard offerings. Logical pairings include those with other sporting goods—type merchandise and services, such as Willy's Sports Shop and Taxidermy in McGregor and Lake Scandi Bait, Tackle, Gun Shop, and Campground in Glenwood.

That last one crosses the line into the other common-sense bait-plus category: tourism-related businesses (aka places visiting anglers would go when not angling). Wake up from a restful night's sleep at Dassel Motel and Bait in Dassel, and you need not make an extra stop before heading to the lake. Grab lunch *and* lures at the Bait 'N Bite in Ray. Stock up on whichever necessities you require for a day of fishing at TJ Snells Bait & Groceries in Cushing or Lucky Bait & Liquor in Grand Rapids. Some combos defy logic, though, such as OK Tire & Bait in Randall. But does there really need to be an explanation? In Minnesota, it

makes sense to tack "and Bait" to the end of any business. Remember, lakes are everywhere, and therefore so are bait shops.

Bait Shop:

A place that sells night crawlers, minnows, and other things used to lure fish. It may be housed alone or with another business, such as a gas station or cafe.

you know you're in
minnesota when...
... a potluck isn't a potluck without bars

Like hot dish, bars are one of the state's culinary staples not recognized by Webster's dictionary. Pronounced with a subtle piratelike *arrr* and a soft, clipped *s*, bars are a typical dessert here. They are baked in a 9- by 13-inch pan and then cut into squares or rectangles.

Some people will have you think that bars are cookies, but they're not. They are *like* cookies, only uniformly softer and without all that individual dough-measuring. They are also like cake, but denser and edible without utensils. (A brownie is not a bar, by the way. It's just a brownie.) If not being brought to a potluck, picnic, or similar gathering, bars are covered and stored on the countertop in the pan they were baked in.

The dessert is pervasive here, and it knows no boundaries. Toffee bars, lemon bars, chocolate chip bars, fudge bars, apple bars, peanut butter bars, almond bars—anything goes. Some varieties have achieved national fame, such as the seven-layer bar and the Rice Krispies bar. We know some people call them Rice Krispies treats, but in Minnesota they're bars.

Bars:

Resembling a firm cake or soft cookies, these sweets are baked in a 9- by 13-inch pan and then cut into squares or rectangles.

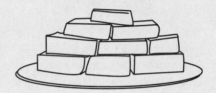

The L.A. Lakers, the glamour team of the NBA, started off in Minnesota in 1947. They were incredible, winning six championships over their first seven years, led by George Mikan, professional basketball's first superstar. But Mikan retired, the team slid, and attendance dropped. The Minneapolis Lakers were sold to Los Angeles, a city with considerably fewer lakes, in 1960.

A couple of attempts to revive Minnesota professional basketball resulted in the Muskies and the Pipers. Each lasted a season; attendance just wasn't there. Then in the late 1980s, the state was awarded an NBA expansion team and Minnesotans showed a renewed enthusiasm for the sport. We named our new team the Timberwolves, for an animal more plentiful here than anywhere else in the Lower 48. The T-Wolves set an NBA attendance record their very first season (1989–90). And not because they were good. On the contrary.

They continued to . . . um, suck for a number of years, reaching an all-time low in 1995 when they set another NBA record— this one for losing at least 60 games for four consecutive seasons. But in 1996 the Wolves nabbed 19-year-old Kevin Garnett straight out of high school as a first-round draft pick. Smiley, bald "KG," as he is affectionately known, kicked off a whole new era in Minnesota basketball. The Wolves

had their first winning record that year and have continued to improve, going as far as the Western Conference finals in 2004.

KG has become one of basketball's biggest superstars, an all-around great player named the NBA's most valuable in 2003–04. He's also an all-around great guy: sweet, well-mannered, wholesome, altruistic—a true Minnesota superstar. Yes, Minnesota basketball has finally recovered that magic combo of talent and spectator mania. If only naming a team for something you have the most of ensured that the combo would last forever.

Basketball:

A game that Minnesotans have recently embraced again, thanks in part to the Timberwolves' NBA superstar, Kevin Garnett.

you know you're in
minnesota when...
... Betty Crocker is considered a local

Minnesotan Miss Crocker has weathered the years fantastically. Her short, dark hair is always neat. Her red top is always well-pressed and accented with a touch of white, such as a scarf or classic strand of pearls. It even looks as if she's peeled off a few years since her first portrait in 1936. But that's the benefit of existing as a marketing concept that gets an official makeover every decade or so. You always look comfortably stylish and put together.

Betty was created in 1921 to personalize responses sent from Gold Medal Flour to customers who had submitted questions about baking and cooking. There was a time when she received up to 5,000 letters a day, including marriage proposals, and was considered the second most recognizable woman in America (behind Eleanor Roosevelt).

Betty was the brainchild of the Washburn Crosby Company, and as such was the face of Minneapolis's flour heyday at a time when the city was the flour-making capital of America. Washburn Crosby and Pillsbury were the biggies among the 20 mills that lined the Mississippi near St. Anthony Falls around the turn of the 19th century. Washburn became General Mills in 1928; General Mills acquired Pillsbury in 2000.

Understanding the scope of General Mills today requires only a quick inventory of icons in the aisles of your local grocery store—the Trix Rabbit; Count Chocula; the Hamburger Helper Helping Hand; Poppin' Fresh, the Pillsbury Doughboy; and the Jolly Green Giant. Betty represents the consumer food-manufacturing giant's early flour-making roots. For an in-depth look at those roots, visit the Mill City Museum (612–341–7555, www.millcitymuseum .org), creatively constructed within the ruins of the old Washburn A Mill. It tells the story of flour, and therefore the city, through highly engaging and kid-friendly hands-on exhibits. Of course, you can learn more about Betty there, too.

Betty Crocker:

A fictitious woman created by the granddaddy of the early Minneapolis flour industry to personalize baking and cooking responses sent from Gold Medal Flour.

A lot of things come to mind when one hears the word *Minnesota*. Biking is not the first. But not only do we lead the country in cold weather and lakes, we lead it in bike-trail miles, too. As of this printing, we're at an estimated 1,500 and counting.

They're all over the place. City, county, and 16 state-owned trails showcase the northwoods, the lake country, Lake Superior, the bluffland, the prairies, and even farmland, plus our metropolitan cities and little towns. Many also include bridges and other cool railroad remnants. (We were among the first in the country to start laying down bike trails where train tracks once stretched.)

The newest state-led project is the Gitchi Gami State Trail, along the popular North Shore of Lake Superior. In the summer of 2005, the first 8 consecutive trail miles connected Split Rock River with Beaver Bay. Eventually the trail will run about 86 miles along the length of the North Shore, from Two Harbors to just shy of the Canadian border, connecting state parks, attractions, and lovely lakeside communities. That will happen sometime between 2008 and 2011.

Bicycle Trails:

Scenic, paved narrow roads designated for bikers. Minnesota has more than any other state.

It can be safely assumed that state residents will use the Gitchi Gami well, as indicated by the love we show to our existing trails. But it's not only us out there. People from across the country find their way to Minnesota to get a piece of the bicycling action, even without our hyping it. If Minnesota someday becomes synonymous with biking, that's absolutely fine. There are plenty of trail miles to share.

What better way to entice a driver whizzing by your town or business to step on the brake than by catching his or her eye with an object three times its normal size? Minnesota has embraced the trend of roadside sculptures wholeheartedly. There's no formal record of this sort of thing, but where there are state-by-state tallies of big statues and world's largest things, Minnesota tends toward one of the lengthiest lists.

What's chosen to enlarge and immortalize is rarely random, so a snapshot of any state's big sculptures tells a lot about its identity. Minnesota's top three big-statue categories—voyageurs, fish, and Paul Bunyan and related icons—are logical in this land of northwoods and lakes. Other icons are equally relevant. With all our Scandinavian blood, no wonder there's a big Viking in Alexandria, a Viking ship in Moorhead, and a large St. Urho (the Finnish saint who reportedly battled grasshoppers) in Menahga.

Minnesota's Iron Range has its big Iron Man in Chisholm, and the World's Largest Ear of Corn in Olivia represents the state's many farmers. North Saint Paul's huge snowman speaks to the state's storied winters. And in Eveleth is another classic icon, one destined to instigate more than a few

Big Sculptures:

1. Larger-than-life depictions of people or things. 2. Type of art found along many Minnesota roadsides.

squealing brakes: a giant hockey stick—one of many subtle social studies lessons disguised as a really cool photo op.

People know about the lakes. And the northwoods. And the farmland. But Bluff Country, in southeastern Minnesota, often comes as a topographical surprise.

The last round of glaciers that crept across the state about 10,000 years ago missed this corner. When the glaciers retreated they emptied soil, sand, and rock into the land they had covered, leveling it off. Their waters drained down into the untouched southeastern land, carving rivers and streams out of the ancient limestone and emptying into the Mississippi. It's called the Driftless Region for having escaped deposits of glacial debris, or drift. But people who know about the area are usually more familiar with its tourism-friendly name, Bluff Country.

Visitors come because the glaciers didn't: The scenery in Bluff Country is gorgeous. Rushing rivers tumble under looming bluffs, and the mass of hardwoods makes it an overwhelmingly popular place to visit in fall. Then there are the cute little towns, state parks, and no fewer than five scenic byways. Any self-respecting Minnesota road-tripper knows about this gem.

The most high-profile attraction is the Root River Valley. The paved Root River bike trail, a former railroad bed, parallels the valley's river for many of its 42 fairly flat miles. (Anyone looking for a bluff-climbing challenge can certainly find it in the connected Harmony-Preston Valley State Trail.) And if you know about the Root River Valley, you know about Lanesboro—a town crazy with adorable shops and bed-and-breakfasts, plus a fruit-centric winery and a quality regional theater called the Commonweal. But don't stop with Lanesboro. There is much more to discover in this surprising corner of the state.

Bluff Country:

A picturesque and surprisingly hilly area in the southeastern corner of Minnesota that is especially popular in the fall.

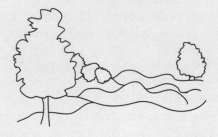

you know you're in
minnesota when...
...you play boot hockey

Only so many people can actually make a living as hockey players. In a state that loves the sport, there are plenty of people who want to do just that. For those who don't make the cut, there are ways to fill the void.

Street hockey, for example. This is nonwinter hockey played in a driveway, alley, or low-traffic street in tennis shoes rather than skates. Participants—most often teens and preteens—block appropriate sewers with old shirts or towels and use what winds up being a hairless tennis ball rather than a puck. Goalie equipment is cobbled together from cardboard, and nets, hauled into the street from separate players' garages, are usually mismatched. (If your net is higher, it's a good excuse for accidentally letting a goal in.) The main disadvantage of street hockey is that if a car needs to get through, the game stops.

When snow falls, rinks complete with boards and lights pop up on frozen ponds. Kids get home from organized hockey, then head straight out for some shinny hockey into the evening. This is also the time when street hockey morphs into boot hockey—street hockey in boots. Play still happens in alleys and driveways, but frozen ponds, lakes, and rinks are better options. (Imagine what a slippery surface adds to the game.)

Boot hockey carries over into adulthood and can range from a group of friends playing a pickup game to actual leagues that play on reserved ice rinks on scheduled days. In the latter case, there are even officials and rules and a trophy awarded at the end of the season. It's nice, in that you build a game-time into your schedule and work toward a championship win—just like the pros.

Boot Hockey:

A winter hockeylike game played with boots instead of skates.

We hear that people on the coasts don't know one Midwestern state from the next. Not so here. Not only do we know where these states are, we also have some serious opinions about them. Especially our neighbors—well, a couple of them at least. North and South Dakota are pretty quiet, so it's hard to size them up. They seem real nice, though.

Iowa's the one we like to pick on. Just ask around. Plenty of Minnesotans know an Iowa joke or two. They often have to do with Iowans' low IQs, even though their state's education system rivals the one we like to boast about. No matter; it's all in good fun. Plus, you can't be too hard on the poor people. They have it rough enough. They live in Iowa, and we all know that the best thing to come out of that state is I–35 North.

But Wisconsin, now, that's the one we have to admit gives us a run for our money. They have the lakes. Not 10,000 of them, but plenty. They've got the northwoods, too. Lake Superior; major sports teams; big, cultured cities—it's actually all pretty familiar. But when it comes down to it, there is one obvious problem with Wisconsin: It's not Minnesota.

Border States:

Minnesota's surrounding states: North and South Dakota, Wisconsin, and Iowa.

11

you know you're in
minnesota when...
...you enter the northwoods

It's about as remote as the northwoods get. Pine trees sprout from rocky islands in lake after lake in the million-plus unspoiled acres of the Boundary Waters Canoe Area Wilderness (BWCAW) in the Superior National Forest, pushed up against Canada in the far northeast corner of the state.

Visitors carry their own food, lodging, and transportation. Canoes are the preferred method of travel, and there are 1,200 miles of routes to explore. A good map and a compass are necessities, as there are no signs in the BWCAW. This is nature at its purest, a place where absolute silence is broken only by the occasional loon call and the gentle splash of a canoe paddle pushing water.

The BWCAW was born with the Congressional Wilderness Act of 1964, which established America's wilderness preservation system. Congress' definition of *wilderness* is an area where "the earth and its community of life are untrammeled by man—where man himself is a visitor who does not remain." Over the years, land was added to the BWCAW and preservation efforts increased. Visitor regulations that follow the "Leave No Trace" principles aim to preserve the area's purity, and permits restrict the number of people in a group as well as the number of groups in the park during peak season (May through September).

Boundary Waters Canoe Area Wilderness:

More than a million acres of unspoiled wilderness, featuring 1,200 miles of canoe routes, on Minnesota's Canadian border.

These lovingly strict controls make the BWCAW what it is—one of the most popular wilderness areas in America, according to the USDA Forest Service, and one of *National Geographic*'s 50 Places of a Lifetime. Each year about 200,000 visitors fill their backpacks, haul in their canoes, break out their compasses, and come to understand why.

you know you're in
minnesota when...
...you travel to The Cities

It's a fair trade. Twin Citians who seek a respite from urban life find it in such greater-Minnesota places as Up North and Bluff Country. And Minnesotans who live outside of the Twin Cities come to the metropolitan area for urban pleasures such as shopping, major league sporting events, and world-class theater.

This is called going to "The Cities." The catchall term, generally used only by Minnesotans who don't live in The Cities, refers not only to Saint Paul and Minneapolis but also to the multiple rings of suburbs radiating from them. The whole area covers seven counties and contains more than 2.5 million people—about half the state's population. Say you visit relatives in a suburb such as Prior Lake, for example, which is approximately 30 miles from either Saint Paul or Minneapolis. You would say that you visited relatives in The Cities, even though you may not have glimpsed even a foggy outline of a downtown skyline.

Do note that in other Midwestern states, "Minneapolis" has the same definition as "The Cities" does in Minnesota. It's even used to refer to Saint Paul and its surrounding suburbs. As you can imagine, this does not go over well with the capital city's residents. Your best bet is to use the proper name of the city or suburb to which you are referring. If you're not quite sure, or if you're purposely being general, play it safe and stick with "The Cities."

The Cities:

Minneapolis, Saint Paul, and the surrounding suburbs, according to Minnesotans who live outside of this area.

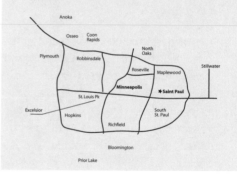

Of course there are designer coffeehouses in Minnesota. Popular national chains have infested larger cities everywhere, and locally owned multi-location operations, such as Dunn Bros., do brisk business as well. In big and small towns alike, unique operations offer the fancy coffee drinker different combinations of steamed milk, foam, espresso, and syrup that start with fresh-roasted and freshly ground beans. These concoctions are not true Minnesota coffee, however.

True Minnesota coffee can be found in the state's church basements, bean feeds, and private kitchens. It comes, preground, in a can and is prepared in a coffeemaker or percolator. The end result should be light brown in color—one shade away from translucence. And it's caffeinated. Always caffeinated. Traditionally it is drunk without milk and/or sugar, though the addition of either is acceptable.

This type of coffee should always be "on," meaning a recently brewed pot should be available, day and evening, to household residents as well as any potential guests. If someone should happen to stop by, he or she should be offered this coffee along with a cookie or a bar. It is not unusual for your last cup of Minnesota coffee to be consumed directly before brushing your teeth and heading to bed.

Coffee:

In Minnesota, a caffeinated and brewed beverage of a light brown color that is drunk at all hours of the day.

you know you're in
minnesota when...
...you still call the department store on Seventh and Nicollet in downtown Minneapolis *Dayton's*

Not so long ago, every city of considerable size had a longtime department store, the kind with elaborate window displays, a fancy tearoom, massive fresh-flower arrangements, and fashionable clothes displayed under coffered ceilings and ornate chandeliers. In Minneapolis that was Dayton's.

In 1902 it was Goodfellow's Dry Goods, downtown on Seventh and Nicollet. As the business grew and evolved, it adopted the last name of its owner, George Draper Dayton. Dayton's became known for its dependable merchandise and class—the Oval Room and its spectrum of chichi designer labels were the epitome of elite fashion in the upper Midwest.

But it wasn't only about shopping; Dayton's was an experience. There was the Oak Grill, a former men's club, all deep red and dark wood and known for its legendary popovers. Dayton's annual flower show was a rite of spring. Its holiday auditorium show, with a new storybook theme each year, became a standard family outing. Both of these seasonal traditions were free. There were other Dayton's stores across the state and the Midwest, but this one, the original on Nicollet Mall, was a Minnesota icon.

Then it happened. In 2001, after nearly a century of business, the Dayton's name came off the grand department store's facade and the words *Marshall Field's* went up in its place. Some shoppers grumbled that things just weren't the same, though many things seemingly remained so. The Oak Grill and Oval Room are still there. The flower show continues, and so does the holiday auditorium show; both remain free. For all practical purposes it's still Dayton's, and people continue to refer to it as such.

The ownership changed a few more times after 2001, and the latest sale instigated talk of another name change. But to many Minnesotans, no matter what the sign out front says, the department store on Seventh and Nicollet will always be Dayton's.

Dayton's:

A beloved Minnesota department store whose flagship location in downtown Minneapolis is now known to non-Minnesotans as Marshall Field's.

you know you're in
minnesota when...
... Deer Opener is practically a statewide holiday

At 6:00 A.M. on the first Saturday in November, about 450,000 Minnesotans in blaze orange are quietly poised in tree stands, armed and doused in doe urine. It's a social thing. Even this part—the communal waiting for that exact moment, a half hour before sunrise, when firearm deer-hunting season officially starts. Deer Opener is a tradition, an opportunity for parents, grandkids, cousins, brothers, sisters, and high school buddies to hang out together all weekend and work toward their shared goal of shooting a deer.

There's a lot surrounding the main event (which is largely a male tradition, thus its nickname, Widows' Weekend). There's the requisite big, hot breakfast eaten in the wee, dark hours. There's the midday break back at the hunting shack, to swap updates, snooze, and catch part of the Vikes game. And in the evening, there are deer hunter suppers—fund-raisers held at the local church, American Legion, or school, where you can expect to eat meatballs and gravy or a similarly hearty meal. Stories and lies of openers past and present fly there and over poker games and at local watering holes across Minnesota.

People hunt for all sorts of things in this state—grouse, geese, even bear. But deer is the big one, drawing in more than $235 million annually. In 2003 Governor Pawlenty decided to acknowledge the big-money tradition with the planned-to-be-annual Governor's Deer Opener. It's the only event like it in the country, modeled after the decades-old Minnesota Governor's Walleye Fishing Opener each May. In the deer version, the governor makes a big show of hunting in a particular area, where he talks to the media about the benefits of hunting and hunters. Clad in orange, he then takes his place in a tree stand at the break of dawn to wait with the other 449,999 Minnesota hunters for that moment when deer season officially begins.

Deer Opener:

The first Saturday in November, when you're legally allowed to hunt deer with a firearm in Minnesota.

you know you're in
minnesota when...
...the noon meal is called dinner

Eating food is a popular pastime in Minnesota, so it's important to understand our dining lingo. The meal served at noon is called *dinner*, or possibly *noon dinner*. The meal served at 6:00 in the evening is called *supper*. Traditionally, dinner and supper look remarkably similar. Each has a main course, such as hot dish or a roast, as well as several sides, such as a vegetable, bread and butter, and Jell-O salad. It can be assumed that both meals will be followed by coffee and dessert, such as pie, ice cream, or bars.

We do have lunch, also referred to as *a little lunch* or *some lunch*. This is eaten outside of regular meal times and is considered to be more of a snack, though it can resemble a meal. Lunch consists of practically anything that's on hand, including sandwiches, cheese and crackers, or reheated hot dish.

Breakfast is served in the morning, of course, unless you're having brunch. That combination of breakfast and lunch is popular in Minnesota, especially on Sunday, buffet-style, following church.

Dinner:

The noon meal in Minnesota.

The game that's called Duck, Duck, Goose in other states is called Duck, Duck, Gray Duck here. This is an easy topic between Minnesotans and non-Minnesotans, a reliable way to fill any void in conversation. There's not much to do besides acknowledge the difference, though, since no one seems to know why it exists.

One theory: The Minnesota version lends a creative element to the game. In Duck, Duck, Gray Duck, kids tend to take the color thing and run with it—purple duck, red duck, black duck—or go far outside the box and use personalized characteristics, resulting in names like glasses duck, ponytail duck, silly duck. (If unsupervised, someone will surely stick a "stupid duck" in there.)

There's also the argument of increased difficulty. Gray duck, the one that signals you're "it," can be harder to pick out among all those other ducks. It's just not as obvious as a goose. Or maybe, just maybe, it's a Minnesota Nice–style technique used to avoid harshly and openly assigning difference, a way to say, "Sure, you're a gray duck. But hey, we're all ducks here."

OK, it's probably just a weird Minnesota thing.

Duck, Duck, Gray Duck:

A popular children's game called Duck, Duck, Goose most everywhere else.

you know you're in
minnesota when...
...you're watching mighty ships in the Great Lakes' top-volume port

When you think of Duluth, you think of Lake Superior. The city sprouted at the southwestern tip of the greatest of the Great Lakes and expanded up and over the 605-foot rocky cliff that frames the water. Now, with a population of 86,000, it's one of Minnesota's largest cities. It bridges the gap between urban and outdoorsy with universities, tall buildings, and high-class restaurants, as well as parks, streams, and that big, blue lake.

The Dakota and the Ojibwe were here when explorer and trader Daniel Greysolon, Sieur du Lhut traveled across Lake Superior and claimed much of northern Minnesota for France in 1679. A fur-trading post on the St. Louis River, one of the lake's largest tributaries, spilled over into a city that was named for him. Duluth's initial glory days came in the mid-1800s. There were abundant trees, then the discovery of iron ore nearby, then the railroads. Add the lake, now connected to each ocean, and conditions were ripe for the burgeoning town. Duluth boomed on into the 20th century. In fact, in the early 1900s, the city was said to have more millionaires per capita than anywhere else in the world.

Glensheen Mansion, an incredible leftover from Duluth's millionaire era, is now part of the tourism industry, an addition to the timber, taconite, and shipping on which

the city was built. Tourists love this town—approximately 3.5 million visit it every year. There's plenty to do, but the top draw really is the lake. Waterfront's Canal Park is a great place to spend an afternoon shopping, eating, and watching the massive ships. Some still blow the "long-short long-short" code to raise the aerial lift bridge, though it's just for show. (They have radio communication now.) Atop the ridgeline surrounding the city, you get a panoramic view of the action at this, the top-volume port on the Great Lakes.

Duluth:

A hardy Lake Superior port town that hosts visitors gawking at big ships and serves as an introduction to the North Shore.

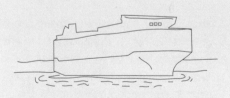

you know you're in
minnesota when ...
... fall is fast and fleeting

Fall is Minnesota's short and cherished pet season wherein timing is everything. We know it's creeping up when summer daytime temperatures mellow out, nights get cooler, school buses reappear, and the air takes on a crisp, smoky-sweet smell. Soon a curtain of color will drop from the northern part of the state on down to the south. You know it's coming when some higher-up leaves trade their green for a more fall-appropriate brown or orange. A random tree may suddenly blaze red or yellow.

Together these are signs that any day, the curtain will hit your part of the state and all the trees will explode in color before they shed their leaves to sport a knobby, naked look. It's a gorgeous if fleeting time, and the beauty it delivers brings with it the quiet warning that winter is preparing to storm the state and settle in for the long haul.

That's just the undercurrent, though. It does nothing to taint our dearest autumn. If anything, it encourages Minnesotans to dive into the year's final snow-boot-free days. We bustle about the state finding excuses to take in the brief color, such as long drives on back roads, bike rides on trails paved over old railroad beds, hikes in state parks, fishing trips on lakes, antiques hunting in small towns, and hay-wagon rides into orchards to pick apples. Tourists lucky enough to arrive at this time enjoy these activities, too. All are different forms of a last hurrah, during which discussion focuses on fall's beauty and when winter will inevitably arrive.

Fall:

A short but glorious time in Minnesota when daytime temperatures are moderate, nights are cool, and deciduous trees display colorful leaves.

you know you're in
minnesota when...
... you can ice-fish from the comfort of your sofa

Minnesotans love to watch the reaction of non-Minnesotans when they point at a sea of white snow dotted with small buildings and say, "That's a lake. There are people fishing in those little houses." The state's most impressive grouping is on 132,000-acre Lake Mille Lacs, where there are usually about 5,000 houses. Even figuring one house, one angler (which is silly given that fishing in the dead of winter is usually a bonding thing), the number of folks on the ice is easily five times greater than the population of any community bordering the lake. This seasonal city operates much like year-rounds do, with streetlights, plowed roads, and public toilets.

Fish-house styles vary. The main requirement is shelter—something to protect you from the elements as you hold your 2-foot pole over a hole drilled into the ice—and it can be as basic as a bunch of cobbled-together plywood. It only gets more elaborate from there. Some structures are bigger and more solid, with notable perks—heaters, beds, a chair that's not just an overturned bucket. There are even super-luxury houses with fireplaces, kitchens, and cable TV, where you can fish from the comfort of your sofa. Multiple fishing lines attached to rattle wheels are constantly in the water, and if it weren't for their ringing when a fish takes your bait, you could almost forget you were out on the ice.

Fish House:

A structure set on top of a frozen lake, within which fishermen drill holes in the ice to catch fish.

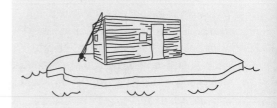

The thing about a fishing derby is that it levels the playing field. There are usually lots of prizes, and you don't necessarily need to catch one of the biggest fish to win one of the biggest prizes. In Minnesota derbies are most often held in the winter as fund-raising events that double as an excuse to stand out on a frozen lake in the company of other anglers of all skill levels. Your entry fee buys you one of the pre-drilled holes, from which you fish during an allotted period of time, usually a few hours. If you catch a fish, you get it weighed in and keep trying.

The awards process varies. At the annual Brainerd Jaycees' Fishing Extravaganza, held each January on Gull Lake, anglers win more than $150,000 in prizes for the 150 heaviest fish caught. Here's the thing, though: Prime prizes are linked to different places, meaning 40th place might get an all-terrain vehicle while 5th gets an ice auger. About 12,000 anglers show up for this derby, making it the largest ice-fishing contest in the world.

The kookiest derby just might be the Eelpout Festival on Leech Lake in Walker each February, where the ugly bottom-feeding eelpout gets its day in the sun. As one might expect of a festival in Minnesota in February named for an unattractive fish, it's a crazy party, complete with Mardi Gras beads, an auto race on ice, and a Polar

Fishing Derby:

A fishing contest, often held on the ice in Minnesota, wherein prizes are awarded in a somewhat random manner.

Big Winner
Last Place

Bear Plunge. You drill your own hole for this one, and not only are you allowed to use a fish house—forbidden in most fishing derbies—but the owner of the most lavishly strange one wins a prize. The derby is raffle-style here. Catch an eelpout, and you're entered in a drawing for one of thousands of dollars worth of prizes, no matter how heavy your ugly fish is.

minnesota when...

...you're wielding a blacksmith's hammer at Fort Snelling

In 1805 explorer Zebulon Pike bought 100,000 acres of land at the confluence of the Minnesota and Mississippi Rivers with about $200 worth of trade items, a keg of whiskey, and the promise of a trading post. Back then the land was rugged, untamed wilderness. Two hundred years later, in the heart of the Twin Cities, much of it remains undeveloped as Fort Snelling State Park. On a bluff overlooking the park, it's always 1827 as costumed guides continually re-create life as it was for the members of the U.S. military and their families who lived in Fort Snelling, near the trading post Pike promised.

There was a fort, and there were soldiers, but there weren't any battles. When the army set down roots here to police the frontier's edge, its main goal was to break up trade between Native Americans and pro-British Canadian fur traders by controlling their route: the rivers. Remote Fort Snelling became the most happening spot on the Mississippi until the frontier pushed farther west in the 1850s.

One hundred years later, development threatened what was left of the fort, but Minnesotans rallied and saved it. In 1960 Fort Snelling became the state's first designated National Historic Landmark, and now it's one of the state's top destinations.

When you enter the fort, you're supposed to imagine that you're a frontier traveler fresh off a Mississippi River steamboat, then wander around as everyday fort life happens. Ask questions of the costumed guides representing the gamut of fort residents and visitors, including Native Americans, fur traders, soldiers, doctors, and cooks. Their answers come straight out of 1827. Participate, too, by helping the blacksmith pound glowing-hot metal, making sure the cannon fires correctly, or smelling the stew. Afterward, hike down to the park and, from between the Twin City skylines, imagine the wilderness for which Pike first bartered.

Fort Snelling:

A fort, set up on the confluence of the Mississippi and Minnesota Rivers, to which the state's first residents came; now a popular Twin Cities living-history destination.

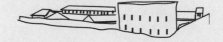

you know you're in
minnesota when...
...you're stuck in a northbound traffic jam on a Friday afternoon in summer

Since the lakes Up North are such a popular destination, one of the most maddening places to be on a Friday during nice weather in Minnesota is on a highway headed in that direction. A lot of people get off work early to try to beat at least the Twin Cities rush-hour traffic, so roads usually clog up somewhere after noon and stay that way through early evening. Particularly Interstate 35. Well, I–94, too.

Traffic jams develop in the middle of nowhere, a bumper-to-bumper nightmare of trucks trailing boats and SUVs loaded with groceries, coolers of beer, blow-up toys, beach towels, sunscreen, sweatshirts, books, and whiney kids. As even Minnesota residents tend to forget, this is also road-construction season. Add surprise detours and reduced lanes to the inordinate amount of vehicles, and you can throw your mileage-to-minutes calculations out the window. It's anybody's guess how long your trip Up North will take.

Of course, people make this trek for a reason. Once you get to the lake, it will surely be worth the white-knuckled trip. The memory of it fades quickly as you dive right into the fishing, boating, and sunbathing. After just a day of your preferred lake relaxation, it's easy to block out what is logical and true: Like you, everyone needs to head home at the end of the

weekend. A similar sort of traffic jam happens in the reverse direction on Sunday. Use this knowledge as a reason to extend your time at the lake by a day or two. The same southerly trip completed on a weekday allows you to better preserve that post-vacation high.

Friday Traffic Jam:

A mass of bumper-to-bumper vehicles on roads headed north in Minnesota during summer and fall, as a result of people going to "the lake."

Minnesotans love golf. Many stow clubs next to their skis in their car trunks through the unpredictable transition from fall to winter, when you never know which equipment you'll be able to use. Everyone in the state has either bragged about golfing on an unseasonably warm December day or knows someone who has.

This sort of supreme dedication has deep roots. The Saint Paul Town & Country Club developed a crude course back in 1893, at a time when American interest in the sport was chiefly on the East Coast. Today the club's course is one of the oldest in the nation still on its original site—second only to Shinnecock Hills near Long Island—and the state has more golf enthusiasts than you can shake a lob wedge at. Depending on the year and whom you talk to, Minnesota has the most golfers per capita. This claim probably isn't that far from the truth. Regardless, the fact that we're trying to prove we love the sport most shows that the love is there, in some great amount.

That love is evident each spring. As soon as the grass peeks through the snow, we start pestering courses for tee times. We just can't wait to yell "Fore!" in the state's hundreds of public and private courses. (Premier among them is Giant's Ridge in Biwabik, which has come in at the top of all

Golf:

1. A game that requires swinging a club at a little white ball with the intent of hitting it into a small hole in the ground. 2. A sport Minnesotans love.

sorts of *Golf Digest* national rankings since opening in 1997.) Though the golf season is much shorter here than it is in more southerly states (aka most states), these courses still see plenty of play given that a healthy percentage of Minnesota's population is perpetually waiting for the right time to sneak in a round. Random car-trunk checks would prove this.

you know you're in
minnesota when...
...you associate positively with the word *gopher* (but don't quite know why)

Minnesota's nicknames include the North Star State, the Land of 10,000 Lakes, and the Gopher State. Given that we're located in the north and have lots of lakes, these first two make sense. Ask Minnesotans why their state is named for a burrowing rodent, though, and most will admit ignorance. Rightfully so, since there are varying accounts to explain this term. And the one that seems to get the most credence is kind of long.

Apparently, in the mid-1800s, before Minnesota was even admitted to the Union, people started arguing about the all-important question of what animal should represent their prospective state. Some said beaver; some said gopher. The beaver people thought the gopher undignified and kind of mean, and the gopher people thought the beaver too sparse (compared to the gopher, anyway).

Then in 1858, with this pressing issue unresolved, Minnesota became a state. The beaver/gopher debate was overshadowed by a bigger topic: railroads. We needed them. After much debate, Minnesotans voted to allow the legislature to float some railroad companies $5 million to make it happen. They took the money but didn't finish the railroads.

A satirical cartoon depicting gophers with human heads pulling a rail car ran in news-

Gopher:

1. A burrowing rodent. 2. A state symbol. 3. A player on a University of Minnesota sports team.

papers across the state. Evidently this cartoon really hit home. The humanized gophers were wearing top hats to represent bigwigs (likely politicians or the railroad executives). The logic goes that as gophers eat farmers' crops, these bigwigs ate the state's money. The beaver idea fell to the wayside. Gopher State it was—though it's unclear why Minnesotans would want to be named for the people who cheated them.

Regardless, the state university promptly picked up the name for its sports teams and mascot. Fans continue to cheer "Go, Gophers!" at popular U of M sporting events, long after the mascot's significance faded into oblivion along with, thank goodness, that silly beaver idea. "Go, Beavers"? Come on.

Minnesotans believe in live theater. They support many great playhouses around the state, but the Twin Cities are where people can, and do, show up in really big numbers. And those people love to toss around this fact: The Twin Cities have more theater seats per capita than any major city outside of New York.

Preeminent among all Minnesota (if not all Midwest) theaters, big and small, is the Guthrie. The commercialism of Broadway drove director Sir Tyrone Guthrie to Minneapolis in 1959. His dream: a nonprofit theater with resident actors performing the classics. The heartland seemed like a good place to root this then-unique approach to theater, and the Twin Cities in particular were appealing because of their support of the arts, many colleges, and great enthusiasm for Guthrie's idea. The Ralph Rapson–designed space opened in 1963 with a production of *Hamlet*.

Over the years the Guthrie stayed true to its creator's vision, developing an international reputation in the process. Classic works from playwrights including Anton Chekhov, Tennessee Williams, and W. Somerset Maugham have graced its thrust stage. A work by Shakespeare is a standard nearly every season, as is Charles Dickens's *A Christmas Carol*, a reliable holiday tradition. The theater's occupied seats aren't the only indication that it is doing things right. The Guthrie received a Tony Award for outstanding contribution to American theater in 1982.

In 2006 the Guthrie will move into a new blue-metal, contemporary $125 million building, its exterior silk-screened with images of the theater's past works, on the Minneapolis riverfront. There will be plenty of space for the Guthrie's staff, as well as classrooms to accommodate the theater's vigorous student outreach program. And there will be three—count 'em, three—theaters: a 700-seat proscenium theater for contemporary plays, a 250-seat flexible studio theater for new and developing works, and a 1,100-seat thrust theater for the Guthrie's standard classical fare, thus securing our favorite theater-seats-per-capita stat for the long haul.

Guthrie Theater:

An internationally known performance theater in Minneapolis and the cornerstone of the state's historically well-funded and -attended theaters.

Minnesota's hockey high point has been called the greatest sports achievement of the 20th century. It was at the 1980 Winter Olympics, when the Cold War was still frigid and Russian Army soldiers skated for the Soviet team, considered the best in the world. More than half of the young players on the U.S. hockey team were Minnesotans, as was Coach Herb Brooks. It was all but a certainty: The young American college boys would be crushed. But as the clock ran out on a dramatic game, the U.S. led 4 to 3. Seconds remained when broadcaster Al Michaels declared, "Do you believe in miracles? Yes!"

Minnesota's hockey low point came in 1993 when owner Norm Green moved the North Stars, our professional team for 26 years. To Dallas, no less. Understand, Minnesota is the State of Hockey. We've been playing the sport on our frozen lakes for more than 100 years and have cheered on our amateur and professional teams for about as long. We strap our kids into skates as soon as they can walk. High school hockey tournaments are practically a statewide holiday. The Gopher hockey team has won the NCAA championship no fewer than five times, under Coach Herb Brooks for three of them. For cripes sake, we're home to the United States Hockey Hall of Fame (in Eveleth). Yet nothing changed the sad truth in 1993: Minnesota had no professional hockey team.

It was a dark time. The days of the green and gold, of Neal Broten and J. P. Parise, of the Met Center—all gone. Then lo and behold, in 1997 we were awarded an NHL expansion team. The world made sense again. The Wild played their first game in 2000 and packed the brand-spankin'-new Xcel Energy Center, built just for them. If you want to see a game, good luck. When there's not an NHL lockout, the stadium is always sold out—16,500 of the 18,064 seats were bought up by season ticket holders. But you can still experience Minnesota hockey at its best. Just go rent the movie *Miracle*.

Hockey:

1. A game played in skates on an ice rink, the object of which is to drive a puck into the opponents' goal. 2. The unofficial Minnesota state sport.

you know you're in
minnesota when...
...you have a Homer Hanky somewhere in your house

No one expected it to happen. In 1987 the Minnesota Twins came out of nowhere to win the West Division, capture the American League Championship, and then meet the St. Louis Cardinals in the World Series. Led by heavy-hitters Kent Hrbek and spunky, lovable Kirby Puckett, the team took the series, winning Minnesota's first major league championship since the Lakers in 1954.

The fans were there in force, packing the Metrodome and madly, if ironically, waving their little white flags. Homer Hankies—white cloths printed with a baseball logo, introduced by the *Star Tribune*—were born to support this team of underdogs. It was the perfect way for mild-mannered Minnesotans to show their support.

The Twins came to town in 1961 as the state's first major league baseball team. Despite a few brushes with greatness, including winning an American League pennant and hosting career Hall of Famers Harmon Killebrew and Rod Carew, the team generally was not seen as a major threat. But then came 1987. Just three years later the Twinkies had dropped to last place, but they came back to win the World Series for the second time in 1991. Again the Metrodome was a sea of waving white.

Today's Twins are still the underdogs of sorts. They have one of the lowest payrolls

Homer Hanky:

A piece of white cloth waved in the air by Minnesota Twins fans to encourage a home run.

in the majors—it's less than a quarter that of high-profile franchises such as the Yankees. Still, the Twins' impressive minor league system produces great players who overlook the (relatively) low salary and outdated stadium (which, with its infamous Hefty bag–style fence in right field, was never suited for baseball in the first place). We're actually considered one of the organizational talents—a small-market David against MLB's famous Goliaths. We win. Not the World Series lately, but central division titles in 2002, 2003, and 2004. And as the team has proved in the past, anything could happen. You never know when Homer Hankies, reserved for the playoffs and beyond, will wildly wave in large numbers again.

you know you're in
minnesota when...
...you eat hot dish

Hot dish is a complete meal baked in a shallow 9- by 13-inch pan. It's a cheap, quick, and easy supper option, being that many of its ingredients, such as the requisite cream of mushroom soup, come out of a can. Other common components include ground beef, peas, beans, stewed tomatoes, noodles, and crunchy toppings made of French-fried onions, corn flakes, or crushed Saltines.

Though there are tried-and-true recipes, such as Tuna Noodle, Green Bean, and Tater Tot Hot Dish, the meal's construction is an adaptable art. The veteran assembler with a well-stocked pantry can whip one up at a moment's notice, effortlessly rounding out the dining experience with buttered bread and/or pickles. (This person also probably owns at least one piece of hot dish paraphernalia, such as an insulated carrier designed for failsafe transportation to a potluck.)

Cooks have always thrown whatever is readily available into hot dishes, which is why people from northern Minnesota tend to have at least one standard in their repertoire featuring wild rice. For those in the state's Red River Valley, it's potatoes, and if you've ever lived near Austin, you probably know one recipe containing SPAM.

In other parts of the country, hot dish is commonly called casserole.

Hot Dish:

A hot meal baked in a 9- by 13-inch dish, often including ground beef, vegetables, noodles, and cream of mushroom soup.

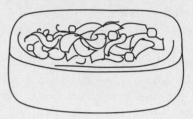

you know you're in
minnesota when...
...you're bowling with a frozen turkey

International Falls, whose downtown provides a view of Canada right across the Rainy River, is the place that people in the Lower 48—even much of Minnesota—look to for comfort on extremely cold days. The temperature recorded in this city is trotted out during national weathercasts as a way of saying, "You think you're cold? Well, check *this* out." In I Falls, as residents call it, the mercury generally stays at or below the freezing point from November through March. Below-zero is a regular occurrence, especially when you take the wind chill into account.

The city of about 7,000 uses this chilly reputation to its advantage. I Falls is a center for cold-weather testing of things like car batteries and clothing. It has a thriving winter tourism industry that caters to ice-fishermen and snowmobilers, people who pray for weather like this. And it celebrates Icebox Days, with standard events such as the Freeze Your Gizzard Blizzard Run, a bonfire with ice-skating, and frozen turkey bowling. All this outdoor fun happens each January, when the average daily temperature is about 3 degrees.

International Falls:

A Minnesota city on the Canadian border that's known as The Nation's Icebox.

you know you're in
minnesota when...
...you visit Bob Dylan's hometown on the Iron Range

Northeastern Minnesota is one of those rare places in the state where a "mixed marriage" hasn't always meant one between a Norwegian and a Swede. Hundreds of mining companies set up shop there after the discovery of rich iron ore deposits in the 1880s. Mining jobs were perfect for immigrants with few English language and work skills, and they came from all around Europe, including Finland, Serbia, Croatia, and Italy.

Mining camps across the three ranges—Vermillion, Mesabi, and Cuyuna—grew into communities as these ranges prospered, providing the bulk of the country's ore. The industry peaked during World War II, then hit bottom in the 1960s. (Perhaps this provides some insight on restless folk music legend Bob Dylan [then Zimmerman], who left his Iron Range town of Hibbing during this decline.)

With the ranges fast depleting, University of Minnesota scientists saved the day by developing a process to make use of a low-grade ore called taconite. The tourism industry helped, too, by playing up the Iron Range's roots. Ironworld Discovery Center in Chisholm (800–372–6437, www.ironworld.com), for example, has exhibits on immigration and mining history as well as tours of a working taconite mine and a trolley tour past abandoned open-pit mines. (They're like picturesque lakes now.) At

Soudan Underground Mine State Park on the Vermillion Range, hard-hat train tours take you more than a mile underground for a look at this range's history. At Hill Annex Mine on the Mesabi Range, visitors get boat tours in the water-filled open-pit mine—an educational and startlingly beautiful trip.

There's a lot of beauty in the Iron Range. A peek at the Iron Trail Convention and Visitors Bureau Web site, www.irontrail.org, shows the area with its best foot forward. Besides the mining-related attractions, there's the Superior National Forest, the Mesabi paved bike trail, hiking trails, world-class golf, lakes, and, of course, some Bob attractions in Hibbing.

Iron Range:

The northeastern part of Minnesota, once known for its rich iron ore deposits.

It took a surprisingly long time for European settlers to figure out where the massive Mississippi River began. After several inaccurate "discoveries" of the Mississippi's source, Henry Rowe Schoolcraft finally had the sense to ask the Native Americans who'd inhabited what is now northern Minnesota for thousands of years. It was Ozawindib, an Anishinabe guide, who led Schoolcraft to the site in 1832. Schoolcraft named the lake Itasca by combining the Latin words *veritas* and *caput* (together meaning "true head"), then lopping off three letters from both the front and back ends.

Anthropologist, land surveyor, and historian Jacob V. Brower worked to save the surrounding pine forests from logging, and in 1891 he finally succeeded in his efforts to create Itasca State Park, Minnesota's first. It's also Minnesota's most popular state park, with about half a million visitors coming each year to explore more than 32,000 acres and 100 lakes.

Most people who come check out the headwaters, which were routed and beautified in the 1930s to make sure visitors would encounter a definitive and pretty sight. A nearby paved trail runs by outdoor exhibits and by the visitor center (named for Brower), which has a cafe and gift shop. The destination really is picturesque—the

Itasca State Park:

The birthplace of the Mississippi River and Minnesota's oldest state park.

glistening lake pours across a 12-foot-long ribbon of rocks to officially become the river's first few feet. People peel off shoes and socks and try to balance as they cross the slippery stones or just dip their feet into the shallow, slow-moving waters.

It's meek, even *cute* here, just 4 feet wide at one point. This is in great contrast to the powerful river that later divides the state's two largest cities (Minneapolis and Saint Paul), passes below bluffs hunched up against charming river towns on its southern Wisconsin and Minnesota banks, and then swells along the rest of its 2,552-mile trip through America's heart to the Gulf of Mexico.

you know you're in
minnesota when...
... you're offered Jell-O salad

Jell-O salad is a popular side dish in Minnesota. Take a cue from the name: This is not a dessert. *Plain* Jell-O is a dessert. So is Jell-O gussied up with whipped cream or marshmallows. But as soon as you add a fruit or a vegetable to Jell-O, it becomes a salad and therefore a side dish, perfectly at home alongside the seven-layer and wild rice varieties also common here. Popular Jell-O salad ingredients include pineapple chunks, chopped apples or celery, grated carrots, oranges, and sliced bananas.

It's an extremely easy salad to make, given that Jell-O is just water added to a packet of powder. The salad requires only one more step: Before refrigeration, toss in whatever fruit or vegetable you have lying around. Beware the Jell-O salad rut, where you fall back on the same old combination, oftentimes the ever-popular red Jell-O with sliced bananas. Remember that it's easy to get creative with this dish by trying out various color combinations (or even flavor combinations, if you're one who subscribes to the belief that different shades of Jell-O really represent different flavors). Think green Jell-O with maraschino cherries for Christmas or a Jell-O mold, layered with red and blue Jell-O containing bananas, for July 4. There are no limits or guidelines, except those imposed by your own imagination and bravery.

Jell-O Salad:

Jell-O mixed with fruit or vegetables and served with a meal.

Despite its festive appearance, this is an everyday salad not reserved for special occasions, although family reunions, holiday spreads, and church-basement suppers following a funeral for a very popular person will likely offer a rainbow of Jell-O salad variations. No Minnesota potluck or salad bar is truly complete without this side dish.

The Green Giant was born in Minnesota in 1925 when the LeSueur-based Minnesota Valley Canning Company decided that a good way to hawk its new style of peas would be to slap a huge man wearing a dress and cap made of green leaves on the can.

Oddly enough, they were right. The Green Giant was such a hit that he became a symbol for the entire company, which was eventually renamed for him. Over the years his skin turned green and he officially became Jolly, as proven by the bellowing of "Ho, ho, ho," a well-known jolliness indicator (e.g., Santa). The Green Giant also acquired a sidekick named Sprout, a little fella with a similar outfit who is said to help him grow vegetables.

In 1979 Pillsbury bought Green Giant and, in so doing, gave the two green mascots a giggly little brother in the Pillsbury Doughboy (a puffy white marketing tool made of dough and named Poppin' Fresh). Pillsbury, a longtime Minnesota company that started as a group of flour mills in 1869, moved company headquarters out of LeSueur and eventually closed the town's plant.

Still, the roadside billboard that drivers see as they head into LeSueur proclaims it the Valley of the Jolly Green Giant. It also depicts the Giant and Sprout. That, sadly, is about all that's left of the great green one

here, except for some memorabilia in the small town museum. About 60 miles south of LeSueur in Blue Earth, however, there's a 55-foot-tall Green Giant statue. Though it's not the big guy's birthplace, Blue Earth had one of the earliest Minnesota Valley Canning Company factories, and it still packs and labels Green Giant products.

The giant appears quite comfortable there, not far off Interstate 90. During the holidays he dons a red scarf. Each August he sports a Harley vest to blend in with motorcyclists heading to Sturgis. And in 2006 he'll get his very own museum.

Jolly Green Giant:

A fictitious big green man wearing a short dress of green leaves, created by the Minnesota Valley Canning Company as an agricultural marketing tool.

you know you're in
minnesota when...
... you own jumper cables and you know how to use them

Even the most mechanically challenged Minnesotans develop a specific set of winter-related knowledge pertaining to motorized vehicles. The most basic of tools is the windshield scraper. Everyone has one. Even if you have a garage or a remote car starter that allows you to turn on your engine from inside your home, at some point when you're out in the cold, snowy world, you'll need a scraper. The best is the big kind, with the scraper on one end and a brush on the other. (Though in a pinch, a credit card and some swipes with your arm are good substitutes.)

On the more technical end are jumper cables. Since we know all too well that in cold weather the battery will simply refuse to charge our vehicles, many Minnesotans carry these around at all times. This happens often enough that if a Minnesotan can point out anything under the hood, it's the battery. And if he or she can perform any mechanical task, it's to execute a jump-start by attaching the red and black clamps correctly between a dead battery and a live one.

Then there are the products such as Heet, which we pour into our gas tanks to prevent the gas line from freezing. And 50-pound bags of sand, used to make rear-wheel drive vehicles more navigable in snow. And tricks to get out of being stuck in the snow, such as rocking the car back and forth while turning the front wheels, or shoving blocks of wood or pieces of cardboard under the rear wheels for traction. Of course, four-wheel drive is the best option, but without it, we manage. And for the worst-case scenario, we stash tin coffee cans containing matches, candles, flares, and candy bars in our car trunks and call them winter emergency kits. This is only a backup when, for some reason, our supreme winter-related knowledge just isn't enough.

Jumper Cables:

1. A set of cables that, when attached to a dead vehicle battery on one end and a live one on the other, may revive the dead one. 2. A cold-weather necessity in Minnesota.

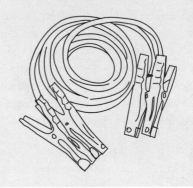

When Minnesotans say that they are going to "the lake," they mean whichever lake they are headed to when they use the phrase. A person goes to the lake mainly in the summer, and it is understood that the activities he or she will participate in while at the lake will largely involve the lake (swimming, sunbathing, fishing, boating, and so on).

You could go to the lake just for the after-noon. We have 11,842 of them—1,000 in Otter Tail County alone—so there's proba-bly one nearby. (We just use that nice, round number in "Land of 10,000 Lakes," a state nickname, because it sounds better.) You could also go to the lake for a week, which is a common way to spend a sum-mer vacation with the family. Some people make this an annual event.

There are lots of "lakes areas" in Minnesota that are known as yearly destinations, including the Brainerd Lakes Area, Bemidji Lakes Area, Detroit Lakes Area, and Alexan-dria Lakes Area. (If you want to sound like a local, call these last two "DL" and "Alex," respectively.) Each consists of a relatively large hub town (featured in the area's

The Lake:

Whichever of Minnesota's 10,000-plus lakes you are headed to when you use the phrase.

name) surrounded by several pretty lakes with resorts. The smaller towns in these areas often have attractions such as cute little knick-knack stores or ice cream shops. They're brief diversions designed to add to your overall experience at the lake.

Note: There is crossover between going to the lake and going Up North.

you know you're in
minnesota when...
...you're awestruck by a view of the world's largest freshwater lake

Sure, it would mess up the five Great Lakes thing, but why not Superior *Sea*? It's the deepest and largest of the five big ones; all the others, plus three more Eries, could fit into it. It's also the largest freshwater lake in the world (if we're talking surface area, not volume).

Superior's oblong 31,700 square miles are contained within two directionally named shores. All of the South Shore lies in America. The only U.S. bit of its other half graces Minnesota. It's termed simply the North Shore, and it's gorgeous. Streams pour down out of pristine forests that halt at the giant cliffs and boulders of Lake Superior's shoreline. When you're standing along this dramatic landscape, looking out on water as far as the eye can see, the word *lake* just seems like such an understatement.

Plenty of things draw people to the North Shore in all seasons, but scenery always figures into the plan. Starting in Duluth, where Minnesota meets Wisconsin, two-lane Highway 61 follows the lake for about 150 miles right up to Canada. The 200-mile Superior Hiking Trail basically parallels Highway 61 along a ridgeline. Inland, there's 2,301-foot Eagle Mountain, Minnesota's highest point, from which you can see the lake (which is, incidentally, Minnesota's lowest point).

Lake Superior National Forest and no fewer than seven state parks line the Highway 61 drive, including Split Rock and its popular lighthouse. Add in quaint lakeside towns, wayside rests, and other roadside attractions like restaurants and antiques shops, and there are always excuses to stretch your legs, whether you're the outdoorsy type or not.

People do swim in Lake Superior in the summer, when the water is warmer than its average temperature of 40 degrees. There's also fishing, canoeing, sailing, and charter-boat rides to bring people up-close and personal with this incredible freshwater lake.

Lake Superior:

1. The deepest and largest of the Great Lakes. 2. The world's largest freshwater lake by surface area. 3. A popular Minnesota vacation destination.

Lake Superior

you know you're in
minnesota when...
...one of the state's most famous towns is fictional

Millions of people worldwide are smitten with the little Minnesota town where "all the women are strong, all the men are good-looking, and all the children are above average." Across America listeners tune in to National Public Radio to hear author and radio personality Garrison Keillor's sighing, rhythmic voice detail the news of Lake Wobegon, in front of a live audience, during *A Prairie Home Companion*.

It's simple news, the kind that develops in an agricultural town of 942 mostly honest, God-fearing, hardworking people who occasionally drink cheap beer in the company of mounted deer heads at the Sidetrack Tap. Lake Wobegon offers a pastoral life both innocent and wise, odd and practical, and without bells, whistles, or strip malls. It's a life that gets harder to imagine with each passing year, which makes you wish that it wasn't pretend.

Well, kind of pretend. For decades people were disappointed by Keillor's assertion that Lake Wobegon is fictional. Then Keillor realized that this wasn't exactly true. He's an Anoka-born Minnesota boy, after all, who helped start a Minnesota Public Radio (MPR) station in Stearns County. There he absorbed the essence of everyday life that would eventually become Lake Wobegon. The first live *A Prairie Home Companion* was broadcast in 1974 at MPR's Saint Paul

Lake Wobegon:

A fictional Minnesota small town with a worldwide following.

station. Today the show has its own home in the renovated Fitzgerald Theater downtown, and a movie of the same name is scheduled for release in 2006.

The folks up in Stearns County are happy for the acknowledgment they always figured they deserved. Visitors seeking Lake Wobegon can glide through the countryside between towns on the 46-mile Lake Wobegon multiuse trail. The annual Caramel Roll Ride, a bicycling event on the trail, combines a scenic workout with a local diner tour. Serious fans should make sure to see Holdingford (population 736), one of two trailhead towns. On his trip to explore the roots of Lake Wobegon, Keillor deemed Holdingford "most Wobegonic."

you know you're in
minnesota when...
... you know the difference between lefse and a
tortilla

Lefse (pronounced "LEF-suh") is a Norwegian thin bread typically made from potatoes, shortening, flour, and cream, though recipes do vary. It's rolled super-thin and cooked on a heated griddle until little brown spots appear on the white dough. The end result looks like a tortilla, but *do not put salsa on lefse.* That's just weird.

Lefse is most commonly eaten as a dessert. Purists will tell you to spread butter on one side of the bread, sprinkle it with sugar, then roll it up and eat. If you're feeling crazy, throw some cinnamon on top of the sugar. You usually find lefse in Minnesota homes during special occasions and holidays, most notably Christmas. Do note: Although lefse is usually considered a dessert, those closer to the homeland eat it buttered with meals and consider adding even sugar a sacrilege.

Making lefse is more difficult than it sounds. Some people have special lefse-making accoutrements such as round griddles, boards, grooved rolling pins, turning sticks, towels, and such. Although the best lefse is made by your Norwegian grandma, companies in Minnesota cater to those without one. The House of Jacobs in Spicer, for example, started when Dennis Jacobs's mom threatened to stop making lefse because the process had become too annoying. Her husband created a pastry board and cover to make preparation eas-

Lefse:

A potato-based Norwegian thin bread that resembles a tortilla.

ier and to ensure the future presence of lefse in the Jacobs household. Son Dennis saw that other Minnesotans could benefit from his father's creation. He started House of Jacobs, which ships lefse and lefse-making accessories across Minnesota and the United States.

Incidentally, the world's largest lefse was made during a centennial celebration in Starbuck, Minnesota (a town with strong Norwegian roots). It took eight people, 30 pounds of potatoes, and a 1,200-pound griddle to make the 9-foot, 8-inch flatbread. Each May, they remember their accomplishment with Lefse Dagen (Lefse Day). Visitors watch lefse-making demonstrations, build their own lefse, and, of course, eat the potato-based thin bread.

A good pair of long underwear is a necessity in Minnesota, even if you're not a fan of outdoor wintertime activity. During a summer trip Up North, for example, it's usually a good idea to pack long underwear alongside your bathing suit. Once the sun sets, things can cool down enough that the extra layer, along with a bonfire, will keep you just comfortable. And because winter temperatures get as low as they do, eventually you'll see the benefit of insulation—even if you're not cross-country skiing or snowmobiling, but just walking from the parking lot to the grocery store. A mail carrier and an office worker are each as likely as an outdoor sports enthusiast to break out the long underwear in November and wear it right up to spring.

Advancements in long underwear make this a much more streamlined and comfortable practice these days. New thin, body-hugging, synthetic fabrics insulate as well as or better than the old scratchy, bulky, natural-fiber type, while offering the added benefits of wicking away sweat and drying quickly. Note that these are not the typical undergarment features touted at your local Victoria's Secret. Even in Minnesota in the dead of winter, you're not going to see storefront-window mannequins sporting the latest in sexy, head-turning long underwear fashions. Still, it is underwear—it just covers a larger area than the regular type. Considering that it's an inevitable staple here, Minnesotans have no choice but to assign it a mystique similar to that of lingerie.

Long Underwear:

Clothing, often made of a synthetic fabric, worn against the skin as an extra insulating layer at all times during cold winter months.

you know you're in
minnesota when...
...a loon cry floats across the lake

Even when they're silent, they're amazing to watch as they float in the water with their black-and-white speckled plumage, red eyes, and black heads that gleam green in the sunlight. But then comes the lonely howl that rises and drops, and then the haunting, bobbing flutter. The calls sound ancient, and in a sense they are—the common loon dates back 60 million years, making it one of the oldest living bird species in the world. When its sad and beautiful sound floats across a quiet lake at dusk, it completes a moment that felt full, until then. It just makes sense.

One of the best things about this experience is that it's common—common enough for the Minnesota legislature to deem the loon our state bird in 1961. We have more loons than any other state in the Lower 48, about 12,000 at last count. They're most often found in Minnesota's northern two-thirds on clear, fish-filled lakes. You'll see them alone, in pairs, or traveling with a baby or two. If you're really lucky, you'll catch a chick riding on a protective parent's back.

Usually you don't have to do anything out of the ordinary to glimpse a loon. You'll see one while you're canoeing or fishing or gazing out onto the lake from the end of a dock. It's part of the entire Minnesota lake-vacation experience—wet swimsuits, fish fries, card games, mosquitoes, sweatshirts that smell of bonfire smoke, and loon cries that drift across the lake on a starry night.

Loon:

1. A bird with a black head and black-and-white spotted body that floats on lakes, dives for fish, and has a warbling call. 2. The Minnesota state bird.

It smells. That's the most distinctive characteristic of lutefisk, a traditional Norwegian dish of dried codfish soaked in lye. Next on the list: its consistency, which has been compared to Jell-O. Needless to say, something that can be described as stinky fish Jell-O is a bit of a public relations challenge. The hardy Scandinavians who consider the fish a tradition are dying off, and younger folks are failing to pick up the lutefisk-eating habit in any large numbers.

But the dish is not in danger of extinction any time soon. Churches across Minnesota hold annual lutefisk suppers, open to the public, where the fish is most often served in the traditional manner—baked and topped with butter, salt, and pepper. Plenty of the Minnesota-based companies that supply lutefisk to the suppers also ship to private buyers around the country, particularly during Christmas, when nostalgia for the traditions of old runs high.

The Olsen Fish Company in Minneapolis, for example, sells about 500,000 pounds of the stinky stuff each year, making it the largest processor of lutefisk on the continent. (Its best seller is actually pickled herring, another stinky fish with an interesting consistency that Scandinavian Minnesotans love.) The company has a toll-free Lutefisk Hotline, and its motto is "Love that Lutefisk"—a phrase it hopes more people

Lutefisk:

1. A Norwegian dish of dried codfish soaked in lye. 2. One of several stinky fish with a strange consistency eaten by hardy Minnesotans.

will take to heart. To aid in this process, Olsen stresses that the gelatinous texture of lutefisk comes from overcooking and is therefore easy to avoid. The smell, though—that's something you'll have to live with.

you know you're in
minnesota when...
...everyone knows a Lutheran

When you see a white steeple rising above a crop field in the Minnesota countryside, there's a good chance it belongs to a century-old Lutheran church. Most of the state's first European settlers were Germans, Norwegians, Swedes, and Danes, most of whom followed the teachings of Martin Luther. They brought their religion from their homeland and set up the churches that were cornerstones in developing communities across the state. The settlers established schools, too. There are no fewer than seven Lutheran colleges in Minnesota, with names like St. Olaf (a king of Norway) and Gustavus Adolphus (a king of Sweden). This strong Lutheran base remains today. According to the Evangelical Lutheran Church, Minnesota has the country's highest population of Lutherans.

Given that the religion is tied tightly to the development of the state, a lot of Minnesotan stereotypes are Lutheran stereotypes—the down-to-earth, nonconfrontational manner; the love of weak coffee, Jell-O salad, and hot dish. Of course the Lutheran faith is much deeper than general personality traits and food preferences. To further investigate what it means to be Lutheran in the nation's most Lutheran state, you can always attend a church service, which, much like the typical Minnesotan, tends not to be very showy or noisy (outside of the frequent

Lutherans:

People who adhere to the Lutheran religion; there are more in Minnesota than in any other state.

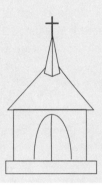

hymn-singing). Or when you're driving by one of those country churches, look for signs advertising its church supper. The coffee will be weak and plentiful and the food homemade. As any Minnesota Lutheran will tell you, that's the way it's done here in God's Country.

Suburban growth triggered the 1952 development of Southdale, America's first enclosed mall, in the Minneapolis suburb of Edina. The Dayton family was behind this project, not surprising considering the family's famed Minnesota department-store past. The Daytons recognized that both convenience and protection from inclement weather would a happy shopper make.

The state continued the tradition of groundbreaking consumerism with the Mall of America (MOA), a 4.2-million-square-foot behemoth in Bloomington, another Minneapolis suburb. Completed in 1992, the Mall of America is the largest enclosed shopping center in the United States—like Southdale on growth hormones.

There's no denying that The Mall is a big deal. It's one of the top vacation destinations in the entire country. Let me rephrase that: People from around the world use their precious vacation time to fly to Minnesota and hang out in this megacomplex. This is not only because Minnesota doesn't have sales tax on clothing, though that sure doesn't hurt. On top of the 4 miles packed with 520-plus shops and four department stores, the MOA has a theme park, a 1.2-million-gallon aquarium, a college, a chapel, fancy restaurants, and a 14-screen movie theater.

A planned expansion would more than double the size of the existing mall with additional shops and restaurants as well as hotels, a casino, and a golf course. The only way the state could top that one would be to create a mall that actually *is* a suburb.

Mall of America:

A 4.2-million-square-foot indoor mall—the largest in America—in Bloomington, Minnesota.

MALL OF AMERICA

These doctor's kids done good. Minnesotans William J. and Charles H. Mayo grew up watching, even assisting, their dad, William Worrall Mayo. After med school, the brothers returned to Rochester to work in their father's practice. The two came up with a remarkable idea: Why not take time to thoroughly examine patients, make sure each receives swift care by a specialist, and always find ways to improve diagnosis and treatment?

This was groundbreaking stuff in the late 1800s, and by 1919 the Mayo Clinic had emerged as a world leader in medical specialists and their schooling. In the wake of this success, the brothers scrapped their partnership for what's become the not-for-profit Mayo Foundation, in which all doctors are salaried and all profits go toward education, research, and patient care. Over the years Mayo has pioneered medical developments such as open-heart surgery, hip replacement, and CT scans. Doctors and patients from around the globe travel to the Mayo Clinic for education and treatment. Mayo doesn't specialize; treating absolutely any illness is its specialty.

The clinic has grown beyond its Rochester campus, where it dominates the city of about 93,000 (though IBM offers its fair share of white-collar jobs as well). This is the only significant Minnesota skyline south of the Twin Cities. Rochester is big enough to have a Super Target and an 11,000-seat Civic Center, which hosts concerts, proms, and meetings. It bears the Mayo name.

Mayo really is everywhere—the historic brick and new glass-and-steel clinic buildings, the founders' dignified mansions, the stately homes of Pill Hill (a pretty, hilly neighborhood where doctors often live), and the plethora of temporary housing for the clinic's 320,000 annual patients (Rochester has as many hotel rooms as Minneapolis). It's a vacation-worthy city, for Mayo attractions and more. And while ideally all visitors to Rochester would be in good health, it's nice to know that when they're not, Mayo will do everything possible to change that for the better.

Mayo Clinic:

A world-renowned medical facility in Rochester, Minnesota.

minnesota when...

... you plan an annual four-day family getaway in late October, when the kids are off from school

MEA, the third Thursday and Friday of October, is a statewide school break that Minnesotans can count on. It's reliable like Thanksgiving and Christmas break, but it has more in common with spring break in that it's not attached to a larger holiday. This leaves the long weekend totally open. Families plan a four-day vacation, as popular Minnesota destinations expect them to. Lodging rates that go down after Labor Day weekend often jump back up to peak just for little old MEA.

MEA *is* attached to teacher conferences. On the two weekdays Education Minnesota, the state's largest education organization, holds a "professional development event for educators" with speakers, workshops, and celebrity and author readings. It's free and open to the public, but most people don't know this. Even if they did, how many Minnesota families would forgo a long weekend at the lake for an educational conference? Even most teachers, who are not paid to go to the conference, choose the vacation.

So, why is this break called MEA? Habit. It was MEA when the Minnesota Education Association hosted the conference. (See the *M* and the *E* and the *A* there?) But in 1998 the association merged with the Minnesota Federation of Teachers to form Education Minnesota. The conference name

MEA:

An annual long weekend for students, during which educators ostensibly attend a professional development event.

changed to the Education Minnesota Professional Conference, but most people just won't let go of the familiar old title—yet. Education Minnesota is still trying to retrain them. No matter. A vacation by any other name is still a vacation.

If you love gambling and you love meat, do Minnesota bars have the thing for you. Two words: meat raffle.

No delusions here. A meat raffle is exactly what you would assume it to be, given the name: a raffle in which the prizes are items such as wieners, chicken, ham, sirloin, turkey, roasts, even lobster tails or shrimp. You know, meat. The process varies, but oftentimes patrons fork over a dollar a ticket, with 30 tickets sold for each product. Then a number is drawn or a wheel is spun, and the lucky ticket holder scores a future night's meal. Either the round is designated to a specific piece of meat or the winner may select from an array of frozen prizes.

This process continues into the evening, until all the meat is spoken for. One can only imagine how many Minnesotans, after a boozy night on the town, have stumbled into the kitchen for a glass of water, then tried to remember where in the world that pack of maple-smoked breakfast sausages on the counter came from.

Meat raffles are not hard to find in Minnesota. Some bars reserve them for special occasions, but many hold the carnivore's ultimate game of chance weekly, or even bi- or tri-weekly. Ask around, or simply look for large plastic signs that say MEAT RAFFLE

Meat Raffle:

A contest often held in Minnesota bars, wherein different types of meat are awarded to lucky raffle ticket buyers.

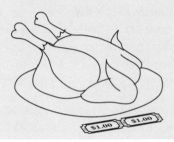

outside bars across the state, including those in urban areas. If it helps assuage concerns of hedonism—Beer! Gambling! Meat!—you should know that the money usually goes to a good cause.

you know you're in

minnesota when...

...you're eating breakfast in a historic dining car at 2:00 A.M.

Mickey's Diner in downtown Saint Paul could skate by on looks alone. It's a cute little Art Deco, pale-yellow and cherry-red 1930s train dining car—all quaint and retro, with rounded corners and neon and chrome. It has graced the big screen in no fewer than four major motion pictures, including *The Mighty Ducks* and *Jingle All the Way,* as well as the pages of publications such as *Smithsonian, National Geographic,* and *Playboy*.

But this place has style *and* substance, and not just the kind it takes to make the National Register of Historic Places (which it did back in 1983). This is the kind of character you get when you mix straight-talking waitresses with the full spectrum of society 24 hours a day, seven days a week, in a narrow space with 18 stools and four booths. Drunk college kids, disheveled transients, suburban sightseers, suit-wearing businesspeople, and even the occasional celeb, such as Arnold Schwarzenegger or Bill Murray—all rub elbows in this tiny diner at the foot of the city's skyscrapers. (Julio Iglesias even serenaded customers here once.) All are subject to the same no-nonsense service that dictates that your order be placed quickly and simply, as soon as your server is good and ready for it.

To top it off, Mickey's does diner food right. Most cooks behind the grill have been there for a decade or two (or three), and their expertise is complemented by the skills of one of the original owners' grandsons, who packs a Culinary Institute of America degree. The entire menu is available anytime, and it offers basics like hamburgers with greasy fries as well as pancakes made from scratch (Mickey's recipe dates to before World War II), baked beans, and other items. The meals are cheap, too, especially when you factor in the one-of-a-kind ambience that comes with them.

Mickey's Diner:

A historic Art Deco 24-hour dining car in downtown Saint Paul.

Minneapolis is the state's cultural capital. Downtown unfolds west of the Mississippi River into a mass of glass and steel buzzing with ad execs, techies, and financial advisors by day, some of whom stick around for the nightlife. There's plenty, including two major league stadiums, the Target Center and the Metrodome; the nightclub-packed warehouse district; the Hennepin Avenue Theatre District; and First Avenue, the state's best live music club, made world-famous by Prince in *Purple Rain*. Past these core 100-some city blocks, the city spills out into neighborhoods (Uptown's one of the most-popular, for its trendy boutiques and restaurants) and a pretty and popular chain of inner-city lakes. This is Minnesota, after all.

But back to the Mississippi. The city began here at the falls, the great river's only natural set. Dakota Indians showed them to French explorer Father Louis Hennepin in 1680, and he spread the word, naming them for his patron saint, Anthony. Many years later, around 1837, the east bank of the river opened for settlement. The community of St. Anthony sprang up, and it used the falls to power lumber and flour mills. Squatters did the same on the other side of the river, and when the land became legal in 1852, residents declared their area *Minneapolis* (a combination of the Dakota word for water and the Greek

word for city). The two cities grew, leading the world in flour and lumber production over the next few decades. After some fuss, Minneapolis absorbed St. Anthony in 1872.

It's still called St. Anthony, though, and it's a nice place to stroll around or dine riverside. The beautiful Stone Arch Bridge, built in 1863 for trains servicing the mills, is now a pedestrian walkway linking the two banks. The bridge offers a two-fer: an up-close look at the falls and a premier view of the state's biggest and most vibrant city.

Minneapolis:

This "city of waters" is Minnesota's largest metropolis.

you know you're in
minnesota when...
...saying good-bye is a lengthy process

It's not easy to say good-bye—especially in Minnesota, where it's a rather lengthy, labor-intensive process. First, you announce your intended action as well as its reason, such as, "Well, I'd better get going, then. It's getting late, and you know how I hate to drive in the dark." (Note that you must give a reason; otherwise your hosts will try to persuade you to stay, thus making a lengthy process even lengthier.)

Next, you stand, and everyone else in the room stands, and each person tells you good-bye in his or her own special way—a handshake, a hug, a back-pat. They thank you for coming and tell you to come again soon and to greet the family and to travel safely (even if you're just going across town), and they may even rush to the kitchen to get some cookies or bars for you to take home. Then they all escort you to the door.

At the door there's another brief and communal round of good-byes. Past this point methods vary. Sometimes you are allowed to exit the home alone, but your hosts watch you from the front door or window, waving. (This is the preferred winter method.) Other times, your hosts actually walk you to your car and instigate another round of good-byes, complete with handshakes, hugs, and/or back-pats. As you get in your vehicle, they remain where they are standing and wave, calling out, "Bye, now!"

Minnesota Good-bye:

The lengthy, labor-intensive farewell that caps off visits to Minnesotans.

It's proper etiquette for you to deliver a final wave as you drive away. The waving ends, making the process complete, only when you are out of sight.

you know you're in
minnesota when...
... the state has its own internationally known brand of nice

In 2004, when an anticipated shortage of the flu vaccine was reported, people around the country freaked out. They called clinic after clinic, stood in lines, and even headed for Canada in search of the vaccine. They could have just come to Minnesota. Here state health officials were begging to use their share of the supply, on highly susceptible groups at least— infants, the elderly, and the chronically ill. Even people in these categories demurred, figuring someone else needed it more than they did.

This is a manifestation of the classic definition of Minnesota Nice: a combination of selflessness, kindness, and instinctive hospitality. Some dig beyond these traits and point to passive aggression and confrontation avoidance. True, strangers are more likely to experience the classic definition, and the more you get to know a typical Minnesotan, the more you might start to wonder whether the deeper characterization has some credence.

We never claimed to be a perfect people— just a relatively down-to-earth people with our very own internationally recognized brand of nice. Here it's not unusual for a stranger to wave at you. If your car is stuck in the snow, chances are good that someone will stop and help you out. If you have a baby or you're sick or there's a death in

Minnesota Nice:

Vague term used to describe the outward kindness of Minnesotans, particularly to strangers.

the family, you'll likely end up with a refrigerator full of homemade food. And if you think someone else might need something, remember the flu vaccine example—Minnesota Nice means that people always think someone else is worse off. Don't ask. Just go ahead and take the hot dish over.

Each year, the state fairgrounds offer Minnesota distilled. Over 12 days ending on Labor Day, about 1.7 million people—that's more than a third of the state's population—mill about these 320 urban acres, celebrating the state during summer's last hurrah. Only in Texas, a state whose very name combined with the word -*sized* means large, is there a bigger fair.

The party was established before Minnesota was. At first the fair came to the people, since late-1800s roads and railroads were works in progress. When it came time for the fair to settle down, Minneapolis and Saint Paul competed to provide its permanent home. Minneapolis offered what is now Minnehaha Park for 50 cents an acre, and Saint Paul offered what was then a county poor farm for free. Saint Paul it was.

As agriculture's role in the state changed, what has been dubbed the Great Minnesota Get-Together adapted. You don't need a vested interest in the new combines showcased on Machinery Hill to get into the spirit. Watch a sculptor carve the likeness of Princess Kay of the Milky Way out of a 90-pound block of butter. Admire the way strategically placed lentils and flax depict a striking likeness of the President. Let the kids feed chickens at Little Farm Hands at the Fair.

And there are always the standard nonagricultural elements—Midway rides, grandstand music, fireworks, talent shows, product demonstrations, live broadcasts by local TV and radio stations. And food. The food-on-a-stick thing is huge at the Minnesota State Fair. Since the introduction of the Pronto Pup in 1947, the list of things served on a small piece of wood has grown to more than 40. Look for Reubens, pork chops, alligator, deep-fried candy bars, Sichuan stir-fry, teriyaki ostrich, and, of course, walleye. This serving style is its own portable attraction, allowing you to multitask your way through the statewide party.

For more info on the fair, call (651) 288–4400 or visit www.mnstatefair.org.

Minnesota State Fair:

The 12 days in August when Minnesotans flock to the state fairgrounds to display agricultural prowess, people-watch, and eat many different kinds of food on a stick. Also known as the Great Minnesota Get-Together.

Minnesota is known for its many lakes. Mosquitoes lay their eggs in stagnant or slow-moving water. It only stands to reason, then, that the bug comes with the territory here. From late May until early September, predominantly (though not exclusively) at dusk and dawn, mosquitoes crash fishing trips, hikes, and picnics statewide. There are lots of them, and they can get pretty big, which is why the running joke is that the mosquito, not the loon, should be the Minnesota state bird.

Bites are often preceded by a low-level buzzing sound that stops abruptly, at which point you'll feel the actual bite, not much more painful than a pinprick. (The silence following a single mosquito's buzz in a dark bedroom has to be one of the more maddening middle-of-the-night moments in existence.) In the bite aftermath, a round area of your skin swells, reddens, and begins to itch. Itching lasts for a few days, unless you scratch the bite too much and therefore develop a scab. That lasts longer.

Prevention techniques vary. In the northern woods, where the bugs are thickest, people wear long sleeves and pants and even nets over their heads. Because this style of dress is not attractive during backyard barbecues in the heat of August, folks in cities and towns try other measures. Past methods included "bug zappers,"

devices that lured the insects with light and then electrocuted them, a death that coincided with a buzz, or "zap." This noisy and murderous method has fallen out of favor, replaced by more humane and silent methods such as yard and body repellent sprays. Also popular: the herbal route, which involves dispensing citronella, often via a candle. This method is usually used in conjunction with the oldest ways of combating mosquitoes: the "wave," performed by moving one or both hands quickly about the head, and the "swat," the voluntary or involuntary practice of slapping a bug with intent to kill.

Mosquito:

1. A flylike bug with a slim, tubular, noselike organ that punctures skin to suck blood, causing a small, itchy, red welt. 2. The unofficial Minnesota state bird.

Remember the opening credits for the 1970s sitcom *The Mary Tyler Moore Show?* The final image was a hip, urban Mary Richards standing on a bustling street, tossing her hip, urban beret into the air in a gesture of uncontainable optimism. That street was Minneapolis's Nicollet Mall (the pedestrian type), an 11-block strip of Nicollet Avenue between Washington Avenue South and 13th Street South. It's lined with trees and park benches; packed with restaurants, shops, and bars; and closed to all traffic except city buses.

The Mall opened in 1967 as a way to revive the Nicollet Avenue shopping district, whose attraction had waned when major downtown businesses started moving to the suburbs. The opening of the country's first enclosed mall, also in the suburbs, didn't help either. Nicollet Mall has had its ups and downs over the years, including one notable "down" after the opening of another suburban mall that happens to be the largest in the country. Popularity still varies within any individual year. For instance, the Mall teems with people mid-summer, particularly on Thursday (farmer's market day), but it's pretty desolate mid-winter, when pedestrians opt for the skyway.

Still, Nicollet Mall remains the paved heart of the city. It features the IDS Tower, the state's tallest building. There's a 12-story

Nicollet Mall:

A stretch of Nicollet Avenue in downtown Minneapolis that is closed to traffic, except city buses, and lined with shops and restaurants.

Marshall Field's with a 100-plus-year history, a Neiman Marcus, a two-story Target (as well as the company's world headquarters), an upscale shopping center, a smattering of independent shops, and a burgeoning Restaurant Row. Then there's Mary, immortalized in bronze a split-second before The Toss. Sure, it's a funny-looking rendition of a fictional person, not to mention a marketing ploy by a major cable TV company. But there she is, amid the shoppers and businesspeople and all the storefront displays featuring their own, rotating brand of marketing, perpetually psyched to be on Nicollet Mall.

you know you're in
minnesota when...
... you see the Northern Lights (aka Aurora Borealis)

It's kind of eerie the first time you see them, especially if you don't know what's going on. Streaks of light appear in the sky, then shimmer and swirl, fade and reappear, curl and flash. Sometimes it's a few delicate white wisps; other times it's an unruly explosion of color, but it's always amazing. You get a kink in your neck from gazing up, mouth open, but there's really no alternative. You can't help but watch and wonder. The phenomenon has something to do with magnetic fields and atoms and electrons and such, but, most importantly, it's really, really cool.

Tourism officials laugh at those who ask them to turn on the Northern Lights. The Lights are unpredictable, but Minnesota is lucky to be far enough north that they do regularly appear. The farther north you are in the state, the better your chances of seeing them. It helps to be away from city lights. Still, it's not impossible to get a glimpse of the Northern Lights from a city in the southern part of the state. They're a reward for outdoorsy night owls, those lingering over bonfires and backyard barbecues or taking a walk to the end of the dock for one last glimpse of the Minnesota night sky.

Northern Lights (aka Aurora Borealis):

A luminous phenomenon that consists of swirling arches of lights in the sky.

Trace the obediently horizontal northern boundary of Minnesota east, and you'll run right into it: the state's chimney. A chunk of water and land carved right out of Canada. It's called the Northwest Angle, and it's the northernmost point of the contiguous 48.

Million-acre Lake of the Woods separates the Angle's land miles from the rest of Minnesota, making that 124-square-mile chunk of the state a, um, *challenge* to reach. You have two options: Cross the giant, island-studded lake by boat or plane, or drive through Canada. If you drive, you'll have to clear customs (currently a painless experience via videophone, though who knows what will happen come 2008, when the United States plans to require passports of all who cross the border, Americans and Canadians included). The road is a 63-mile two-laner that's not completely paved. The drive is pretty, and so is the Angle. Visitors who meet the challenge of getting there are rewarded with pristine wilderness and lots of peace and quiet. They're well taken care of, too. Most of the Angle's 100-some residents are in the tourism business.

We have the fallibility of 18th-century cartography to thank for this little beauty. It *seemed* logical when the squabbling Brits and Americans agreed that the international border should run from the northwest corner of Lake of the Woods, then continue west to the Mississippi. One little problem: The Mississippi is actually south of the lake. When the mistake was discovered, the border dropped down to the 49th parallel (now the Canadian-American border's nice, straight western half). The piece of land jutting into the lake went to America. We just need Canada's help if we want to drive there.

Northwest Angle:

1. The northernmost section of America, as a result of a surveying error.
2. Minnesota's chimney.

Minnesotans use the term *ohfur* when overcome with emotion, either positive or negative. For instance, if Loraine's granddaughter is modeling her new puffy-sleeved, lace-collared confirmation dress for the bridge club, comments such as "Ohfur sweet!" and "Ohfur pretty!" would likely fly.

If Loraine's granddaughter had instead pulled out a skimpy, sparkly little above-the-knee number she planned to wear to the junior prom, comments would probably lean toward the vaguely negative, as in a clipped "Ohfur short," or "Ohfur little." If she went on to say she'd be wearing the dress while riding to the prom on her date's dad's John Deere, the granddaughter would likely see a lot of head-nodding and brow-knitting, and possibly hear a "Mmmm" or a plain old "Oh." (Though upon hearing the story secondhand, in front of anyone but Loraine, it would warrant an "Ohfur dumb," or an "Ohfur silly," spoken in a lowered and serious voice.)

Now, if said granddaughter had mentioned the John Deere plan while sporting a floor-length dress, more suitable for riding on top of a tractor, she would likely have been greeted with something along the lines of "Ohfur fun!" or "Ohfur cute!" Unless she lived in a big city. Then a plain old "Ohfur strange" would be appropriate.

Ohfur:

Word that, when coupled with an adjective, makes a complete exclamatory sentence.

Ohfur fun!

you know you're in
minnesota when...
...Ole and Lena are easy targets

If you're in Minnesota long enough, you'll hear a joke about Ole and Lena, a fictional Norwegian Lutheran couple who are not very bright. They are sometimes supported by a cast of characters including two men named Sven and Lars. The joke is often told by doing all character voices in a Norwegian accent. Like the one about when Ole and Lena got married. On their honeymoon trip they were nearing Minneapolis when Ole put his hand on Lena's knee. Giggling, Lena said, "Ole, you can go a little farder now if ya vant to." So Ole drove to Duluth.

You'll probably hear such a joke from an actual Norwegian Lutheran, as members of that group tend to balance out pride in their heritage with self-deprecation. There are lots of stores in Minnesota that cater to the tempered pride of Norwegians and other Scandihoovians, as Minnesota Scandinavians sometimes refer to themselves. The stores are usually packed with products straight from the homeland, such as dishes, table runners, and food, as well as campy T-shirts, hats, magnets, and coffee cups that say things like "Uff da" and "Pray for me, I'm married to a Norwegian." Gran-

ite Falls has not only one such store, called the Valley Troll, but also the annual winter Ole and Lena Days, which includes a frozen-lefse-throwing contest and a lutefisk lunch.

Ole and Lena:

A fictional Norwegian couple who are not bright and therefore are the butt of many jokes about Norwegians.

you know you're in
minnesota when...
...you receive a one-finger wave

If you're on one of the state's two-lane roads, gravel or paved, pay special attention to the drivers of passing cars. Sooner or later you'll receive the one-finger wave, a raising of either index finger as a greeting. You do not need to know the passing person to receive this greeting. It's a manifestation of Minnesota Nice, a casual and friendly acknowledgment of your existence that still takes driver safety into account.

You will likely be well outside of any city when this happens—the urban one-finger wave is a rarity. It is more common, however, in small towns, where people know you're from elsewhere because they haven't seen your vehicle around before.

But your chances of receiving a one-finger wave are greatest on an open stretch of farm-lined road, when you're traveling along at a leisurely pace. The delivery is most often, but not exclusively, made by men on tractors or in pickup trucks. No matter what type of vehicle you're driving, you're welcome to instigate the wave. And by all means, if someone sends one your way, lift your own index finger as acknowledgment.

One-Finger Wave:

The raising of the index finger, from a gripped steering wheel, as a greeting to a passing vehicle on a country road, often gravel.

An onsale is a place where beer, wine, and/or liquor are sold, to be drunk on-site. A commonly used synonym for onsale is *bar*. An offsale is a place where beer, wine, and/or liquor are sold, to be drunk off-site. A commonly used synonym for offsale is *liquor store.*

On/offsales, basically bars connected to liquor stores, are commonly found in the country or in smaller towns. (Some grocery stores and gas stations in Minnesota do sell beer and wine coolers containing 3.2 percent alcohol or less. This version of said drinks, no matter the brand name, is referred to simply as 3.2. Unless pressed for time, most people go to the liquor store for the full-strength stuff.)

The hours for onsales and offsales vary, but rather than list a bunch of hours here, let's just cut to the chase. Bars close at either 1:00 or 2:00 A.M. Some are closed on Sunday because you need a special license to be open that day. There is no offsale alcohol in Minnesota on Sunday. That's right—if you want to sit around and watch the game and have a few beers in the comfort of your own home, you must plan ahead. Or drive to one of the neighboring

states, all of which permit Sunday sales and most of which have more extended bar hours. In the eastern part of Minnesota, this kind of trip is known as a Wisconsin Run, or 'Sconi Run for short.

Onsale/Offsale:

Places you buy beer, wine, and/or liquor in Minnesota to drink on-site or off.

you know you're in
minnesota when...
... support of the Green Bay Packers is considered treason

While in Minnesota you are unofficially forbidden from supporting Wisconsin's Green Bay Packers. Iowa doesn't have a professional football team, and neither do the Dakotas, so the Packers present the only convenient rivalry.

Minnesota Vikings fans have embraced this rivalry wholeheartedly. Packers fans have, too, which is really nice since that's how rivalries work. Some brave souls, visitors or Wisconsin imports, do break the rule by cheering for the Packers in public or by wearing Packers jerseys or possibly a large foam hat in the shape of a slice of cheese (reportedly a common accessory in Wisconsin).

This is not advisable. In fact, try to remember never to wear the colors green and gold prominently at the same time while in Minnesota. Ever. If you're even *thought* to be a Packers fan, you're likely to receive much harassment, usually in the form of pointed sports banter. Worst-case scenario, you'll be subjected to a string of awful jokes, such as "Where do people in Green Bay go during a tornado? To Lambeau Field, since there are no touchdowns there." That's just one of the printable ones. Consider yourself warned.

Packers:

A Wisconsin football team that, as a Minnesotan, you are required to despise.

Folk legends describe Paul Bunyan as so fantastically tall and strong that he had no choice but to live outdoors and become a lumberjack. It reportedly took five storks to deliver him, though it's unclear exactly where they dropped him off. Bemidji, in Minnesota's northwoods, is one of many American cities to lay claim as his birthplace. His final resting place in Kelliher, however, remains unchallenged, possibly because they have the giant mound of grass-covered dirt to prove it.

Big Paul left his mark all over the state. His footprints created our 10,000-plus lakes. The bobber from his fishing pole is a water tower in Pequot Lakes. And his 110-ton granite anchor sits atop a hill near Big Stone Lake in Ortonville. We've shown our appreciation for these gifts—both a state trail and state forest bear his name. And in what is perhaps the greatest honor given to a truly famous pretend person, many really big statues bear his likeness.

In Paul's professed home of Bemidji, he smokes a pipe alongside his buddy, Babe the Blue Ox. In Akeley he crouches down, offering his hand for you to sit in. In Brainerd there's the 26-foot-tall seated Paul originally at the entrance of Paul Bunyan Land on Brainerd's main drag. For more than 50 years, children gathered (cowered?) before this Paul as he greeted each by name. (Parents fed the names to park workers, who radioed this information to a control booth where the person voicing Paul incorporated them into his spiel.) Most kids don't forget the moment they learn that a bearded man taller than their house *knows* them.

That's why there was such an uproar when the amusement park announced its closing in 2003 and the fate of Paul hung in the air. People in cities such as Dallas and New York tried to snap him up, but in the end Paul stayed in Brainerd. He, along with the rest of Paul Bunyan Land, found a new home east of Brainerd at This Old Farm Pioneer Village, ensuring that generations of Minnesotans can continue to totally freak out their kids. Thanks, Paul.

Paul Bunyan:

A giant bearded logger who, legend has it, left his mark all across Minnesota.

you know you're in
minnesota when...
... you're invited to a Polar Bear Plunge

Some say the Polar Bear Plunge is a tradition handed down from the state's Scandinavian settlers, whose winter bathing ritual consisted of sitting in a steamy sauna and intermittently sprinting into the nearest body of water or snow bank. As years pass, however, people pick and choose which traditions to hang on to. One might think that with the advent of indoor plumbing, jumping into a lake in subzero weather might be the first to go.

Therefore, a more logical explanation for the Polar Bear Plunge is a state-specific brand of winter insanity known as cabin fever. When day upon short, cold day limits your outdoor activity, you do start to go a little loony. It is conceivable that, eventually, you might look out at one of Minnesota's many snow-covered lakes and think, "Hmmm. What if there was a hole in that ice? I think I might go ahead and put on my swimsuit and jump into it. Yes, that would be a fine idea."

Then someone else who's been having similar delusions actually publicizes that he or she plans to cut a hole in the ice and jump into it and that, on a certain day, at a certain time (often during one of the state's winter festivals), anyone who feels so inclined may join in. People actually show up. You'd think that the shock of the water would be a wakeup call, causing each Polar Bear Plunger to realize that he or she had finally gone off the deep end and should consider light therapy. That's not the case, though. People partake in Polar Bear Plunges more than once. Some even form clubs whose members do this on a regular basis. They call it a *hobby.*

Polar Bear Plunge:

The practice of jumping into a lake, sometimes through a hole cut out of the ice, in the middle of winter.

you know you're in
minnesota when...
... liberal leanings and a feather-boa-wearing
pro wrestler define the politics

Minnesota is known for being liberal. This is not to say that Republicans don't exist in this state. Minnesota has actually gone long stretches under Republican rule. But our most famous politicians tend to be liberals, including Hubert H. Humphrey, vice president under Lyndon B. Johnson and the man behind the 1944 merger of Minnesota's Democratic and Farm-Labor parties.

The postmerger DFL produced a number of high-profile politicians. Take Walter "Fritz" Mondale, for example. This VP under President Carter had an alarmingly unsuccessful run for the presidency against Ronald Reagan in 1984, in which he won only the District of Columbia and his home state. Another notable is Paul Wellstone, a former political science professor turned passionate grassroots politician who represented Minnesota in the U.S. Senate from 1991 until his death in a plane crash in 2002. (You still see Wellstone bumper stickers here.) And somewhere in the country's memory bank is the 1973 *Time* magazine cover featuring DFL Governor Wendell Anderson in a plaid shirt and khakis holding up a freshly caught northern pike. The cover line read "The Good Life in Minnesota."

Place that image against that of the governor elected in 1998. Jesse "The Body" Ventura arrived at his inaugural ball in pink wraparound sunglasses, a fringed leather

Politics:

Often thought of as liberal in Minnesota because of the state's many memorable DFLers, though the election of a former wrestler is one notable exception.

jacket, and a Jimi Hendrix T-shirt, announcing, "Let's party, Minnesota!" The former professional wrestler and Navy SEAL was hardly a Republican, but he did beat DFL candidate Skip Humphrey (Hubert's kid).

One could only wonder what this election meant was going on in the minds of Minnesota voters. Turns out they wanted something different. When The Mind (as Ventura renamed himself) declined to run in 2002, Minnesota elected Tim Pawlenty, a Republican's Republican. Pundits are predicting a sea change for the Liberal State. Only time will tell. Since Minnesota elected Jesse, we know one thing's for sure: Anything could happen.

you know you're in
minnesota when...
...sweet, carbonated beverages are called pop

Minnesotans use the word *pop* as the generic name for a flavored, syrupy carbonated beverage. It was once called soda pop. Some people shortened this to soda. We shortened it to pop. If you call it soda here, you will be understood, but it will further be understood that you fall into one of two categories.

Category One: You are from somewhere else. Say, for example, you're a server at a cafe in Minnesota and it's Sunday and in come the Olsons, like clockwork, for lunch after church. You're about to write up their order since they always get the same thing, but Mr. Olson waves you over to introduce his visiting nephew. Steve doesn't say where this kid is from, but when the boy tells you he wants a grilled cheese sandwich, fries, and a soda, it's obvious: He's from outside Minnesota.

Category Two: You are from Minnesota but want to be considered worldly. Maybe little Susie Olson's left for college, on the East Coast or something. Most Sundays, Steve gives you an update that indicates Susie loves school. She's making new friends, she's in the choir, and she's using words such as *environmentalism* and *sushi*. Considering this information, it's no surprise to you that when Susie comes home for the

summer, on the very first Olson-family outing to the cafe, she orders not a pop, like usual, but a soda.

So, non-Minnesotans and fancy Minnesotans order soda. The rest of us order pop. Ordering a coke will get you a Coke. Using this term when you mean "pop" is not recommended.

Pop:
A sweet, carbonated beverage.

you know you're in
minnesota when...
...you wonder why everyone else isn't here

Minnesotans, in general, believe that their state is not the most populated one mainly because of the cold. It's not that we don't have respect for what the coasts have to offer—we always root for any of our own who set out for New York, L.A., and the like. They'll probably be back anyway, we figure, once it's time to settle down. And it's important to note that we don't believe our state is perfect. It's just as close to perfect as any reasonable person could expect to get.

Pride-in-State:

A common belief that Minnesota is the best state.

Oh, the irony: Minnesotans consider humility their greatest trait. Therefore, this deep pride-in-state could go unnoticed by the passive visitor. If prodded, however, Minnesotans will expound on the state's natural beauty, relatively safe cities, good education system, diverse supported arts, and pro teams in all four major leagues. What, besides weather, could be keeping everyone from moving here?

Yes, it's the weather. We must regularly put up with subzero temperatures and snow that requires things like windshield scraping, shoveling, unattractive footwear, bulky clothing, and cold-weather roadside emergency kits. The ability to endure these things is a source of pride in itself—and we're better for them. Plus, they keep the riffraff out.

you know you're in
minnesota when...
... the most famous resident musician is a tiny, reclusive man with a thing for the color purple

Prince is an internationally famous Minnesotan who's made his roots known. Even after more than three dozen albums, multiple Grammys, and a Rock and Roll Hall of Fame induction, the diminutive creator of his own brand of funk-jazz-hip-rock-hop sticks pretty close to home. Specifically, in Paisley Park, his home/recording studio in suburban Minneapolis.

Sometimes you have to wonder why. Unlike strapping, fresh-scrubbed hometown superstar Josh Hartnett, for example, the Purple One hardly fits in with your average Minnesotan, what with the makeup and flamboyant gender-challenging outfits and all. His whispery talk of enlightenment and energy exchanges is not the stuff of typical Gopher State conversations. Plus, he's far from the hardy stoic type—more of a pouter who sulks when he feels the local media doesn't *get* him. Perhaps if he were the kind of celebrity you catch in sweats at the local supermarket, Minnesotans might be able to relate to him. He's not.

But the man has made being unique a career, and a long one, at that. Prince was only 26 back in the 1980s when he hit the big time with *Purple Rain,* a number-one movie *and* album. Despite never climbing back to those rarefied heights, Prince has kept his career very much alive, and on his own terms—not a small feat in today's

Prince, aka The Artist:

A diminutive and reclusive Minnesota recording artist with a distinct sound and a penchant for wearing the color purple.

music industry. So, no, your typical confrontation-avoiding Minnesotan is not the type to set Tipper Gore off on a crusade for parental advisory labels on music. Or to take inventive problem-solving to new heights by changing his name to a symbol. But your typical rock megastar also doesn't live in the suburban Twin Cities, as our Artist does. Maybe that's the stubborn Minnesotan in him.

In the 1970s the Vikings played in open-air Met Stadium, where there'd be snow on the ground for more than half the season. Fans zipped up their snowmobile suits, and visiting teams bundled up, huddling around sideline heaters. Bud Grant, the stoic Minnesotan head coach, would have none of that for his players. No long sleeves. No heaters. No complaints.

The team was tough, and at its heart was one of the most feared defensive units in the league, dubbed the Purple People Eaters. Alan Page, Jim Marshall, Carl Eller, and . . . um, that fourth guy. Oh yeah, Gary Larsen. They weren't big by typical lineman standards. But they were fast, not only tacklers but interceptors, blockers, and runners of loose balls for the touchdown. The Purple People Eaters, plus star quarterback Fran Tarkenton and a cold, snowy Minnesota day, meant that moving the ball was a serious problem for visiting teams. These Vikings made four Super Bowl appearances—all unsuccessful, all played in southern cities.

In 1982 Met Stadium became the first modern park to be abandoned. The Vikings and the Twins moved to the Metrodome. It's a different game indoors, and although the Vikings have never re-created such a menacing defense, the offense has shined with stars such as quarterback Daunte Culpepper and wide receivers Anthony Carter, Cris Carter, and Randy Moss. The early stars are remembered—Tarkenton, Eller, and Page are Hall of Famers (the latter is now a Minnesota Supreme Court justice). Marshall still holds the NFL record for consecutive games played (282). Larsen is kind of the Ringo of the Purple People Eaters, but the true Minnesota Vikings fan remembers his name when recounting the fab four that made up one of the toughest defensive units in NFL history.

Purple People Eaters:

Four legendary 1970s-era Minnesota Vikings defensive linemen.

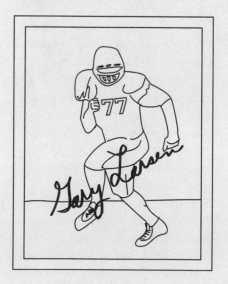

you know you're in
minnesota when...
...Red Wing means more than just footwear and pottery

Both Henry David Thoreau and Mark Twain waxed on about the beauty of this spot on the Mississippi River. It's not their words, however, that draw visitors from around the country to cute little Red Wing, but the three famous products branded for the town: boots, pottery, and stoneware.

At the Red Wing Pottery Salesroom and the Red Wing Stoneware Co., people buy goods directly from the source and watch as they're made. At the Red Wing Shoe Company, Inc., visitors check out a small shoe museum, but mostly they buy boots. The shoe company also owns another of the town's big attractions, the historic, high-class St. James Hotel, established in 1875 and renovated exactly 100 years later.

The hotel is just one of many town draws that don't involve buying something, although you can't talk about Red Wing without mentioning that there are lots of great little shops and antiques stores here. People come from all over the state for the mix of shopping, restaurants (both fancy and folksy), and outdoor activities of all kinds. (Red Wing is only an hour from the Twin Cities, making it a no-brainer quick-fix vacation for city dwellers.) There's a trailhead for the 20-mile paved Cannon Valley Trail, as well as plenty of parks, such as Colvill, known for its eagle-watching. And

then there's Barn Bluff, presiding 350 feet over the city. The hike's quite doable, and once you're up top you can see the area from the vantage point of both Thoreau and Twain and soak in the beauty of which they wrote.

Red Wing:

A scenic, antiques-store-packed town on the Mississippi River that is a popular Midwest getaway destination.

you know you're in
minnesota when...
... you know the sport ringette

Ringette was essentially hockey for girls before there was hockey for girls. Instead of using a stick with a foot to control a rubber puck, ringette uses a straight stick to control a rubber ring. Just set the stick into the center of the ring, and off you go.

There are similarities between ringette and hockey—including the rink, the use of skates, the number of players, and the number of periods—but there are actually more similarities between ringette and basketball. Except that the former is played on ice and without a ball. Okay, let's just break it down this way: There's a lot of required passing in ringette, so it moves pretty quickly. And the players can't check.

The sport was developed in Canada in the 1960s and made its way to the United States in the 1970s. Minnesota embraced it more heartily than did any other state. After-school programs thrived for a couple of decades until the ladies started playing (*gasp*) actual hockey. Women's hockey participation increased 400 percent over a decade starting in the mid-1990s. This decimated ringette. Although the sport still exists, it's mostly played on the national level. The American team often recruits hockey players and usually has more players from Minnesota than from any other state.

Ringette:

An ice-based women's sport similar to hockey, but played with a ring instead of a puck.

you know you're in
minnesota when...
..."road construction" is a season

It's an old joke. Minnesota has only two seasons: winter and road construction. It makes sense. The state's long winters mean that when the roads are not being plowed, sanded, and salted, they're being worked on, in part because of what plows, sand, and salt do to roads. Orange cones are a rite of spring, right up there with robin sightings, tulip bouquets, and street sweepers. The cones pop up on highways statewide with their longtime companions, reduced-speed-limit signs.

At first these construction accoutrements seem innocuous enough. They appear right when the state is released from winter's grip, an event that induces a general giddiness, if you will, among the state's population. By the time this wears off, "construction" is in full swing. Somehow, over the winter, people forget the necessity of building in drive-time for the inevitable road construction. They balk at delays and ensuing inconveniences suffered as a result of detours and slowdowns or standstills, such as being late for work or arriving at a vacation destination an hour or two later than expected. Snow you can conquer with four-wheel drive and well-developed winter-weather driving skills. Construction, though—there's nothing you can do to get around that.

Road Construction:

A season in Minnesota that runs from the end of winter to its beginning.

At least it's usually the shorter of the two seasons. And there is also comfort in the fact that it serves as a handy excuse ("Sorry I'm late. That darn road construction . . ."). Still, it can become maddening. Reference to the fictional season is often an attempt to keep a sense of humor about the situation. This doesn't always work. The joke's old, not magic.

you know you're in
minnesota when...
...Pig's Eye was almost the capital city

Saint Paul is a venerable city. The dignified State Capitol building, the grand Cathedral of Saint Paul, and the stately mansions of Summit Avenue preside over its 70-some downtown blocks, which hold a modest number of skyscrapers. There are just enough of the tall buildings clustered together along the Mississippi River to make the city feel urban. Off its infamously confusing street plan lie major attractions such as the Science Museum of Minnesota, the Minnesota Children's Museum, the Minnesota History Center, and Xcel Energy Center, home to the Minnesota Wild hockey team. But there's a blue-collar air about Saint Paul, a hardworking hominess to downtown's cobblestone streets and sturdy old buildings.

The city's combination of grit and elegance can be traced back to its roots. It all began when the officers at Fort Snelling got sick of squatters hanging around the fort. The displaced squatters headed downriver to start their own settlement. Among them was a fur trader turned bootlegger named Pierre "Pig's Eye" Parrant. He ran a bar popular with Mississippi River travelers. So popular, in fact, that the settlement was called Pig's Eye until 1841, when French priest Lucien Galtier persuaded residents to change the name to the more dignified *Saint Paul,* his favorite saint. The city grew from lumber, fur, and eventually railroad

trades. It became the Minnesota Territory capital in 1849 and then the state capital in 1858.

At its heart is Rice Park, surrounded by three grand turn-of-the-20th-century buildings—the Saint Paul Library, Landmark Center, and the Saint Paul Hotel—plus the glass-enclosed, world-class Ordway Center for the Performing Arts. The city is not known for its nightlife. Still, in the winter, when people leave warm, elegant restaurants for the theater and cross snow-covered Rice Park, with trees draped in white lights, this feels like the best block in the Twin Cities. Classic comfort is what the capital city delivers best.

Saint Paul:

Minnesota's capital and the second largest city in the state.

STATE CAPITOL

In 1885 a New York reporter visited Minnesota during winter. Back home, he reported that the state was "another Siberia, unfit for human habitation." Minnesotans took offense and set out to prove that their state's long, cold winters were not only tolerable but cause for celebration. Out of spite was born the Saint Paul Winter Carnival, more than two weeks of outdoor revelry in January and February, usually the coldest time of the year.

The whole thing is based around the legend of Boreas, King of the Winds, and Vulcanus Rex, Fire King Coal. Boreas is said to have been struck with Saint Paul's awesome wintertime beauty and so declared it his personal playground. His enemy, Vulcanus Rex, didn't like the idea. Boreas reigns during the festival, making appearances with his royal family. Vulcanus Rex and his rowdy crew of cape- and goggle-wearing Vulcans often lurk nearby. In days past they'd paint their faces with soot and plant kisses on the ladies, thereby leaving the black mark of the Vulcan. This tradition has been replaced with the more politically correct practice of asking for permission to draw a black V on a person's cheek.

Most festival activities take place outdoors. There's an ice-sculpting contest, a half-marathon, and, some years, a massive lighted palace constructed of bathtub-size chunks of ice culled from local lakes. The crowning event is the nighttime Torchlight Parade, in which lighted floats, some spewing live fire, wind through downtown Saint Paul streets to the spot where the Vulcans storm Boreas's castle. Fireworks burst over the river, and the celebration begins. See, the Fire King's victory is supposed to signify the coming of spring. Given that it's the beginning of February, it more accurately signifies the midpoint of winter, but c'mon. This is a celebration that involves standing outside in subzero weather while a man in a cape draws on your face. There's no room for practicality here.

Saint Paul Winter Carnival:

An annual Saint Paul festival held outdoors at the end of January and beginning of February for more than 100 years.

you know you're in
minnesota when...
...there's snow on the ground and people are wearing shorts

As soon as we perceive the slightest indication that it's spring—a patch of green, a wayward robin—out come the shorts. It doesn't matter if there is still snow on the ground. Once the thermometer hits about 50, Thinsulate migrates to the basement, short sleeves replace long ones, and we shamelessly bare our pasty-white legs. We're not *trying* to be tough. After a long winter, 50 truly feels not so much tolerable as quite balmy.

Remember, we don't live in one of your cushy states where 50 degrees is a winter temperature. Take 50 away from 50 and you're in the ballpark of what our winters are like. Imagine months of single- or negative-digit temperatures, of seeing your breath every time you step outside, of wearing three layers of clothing daily, of turning your car on to defrost a full half hour before you want to drive it. After that, 50 in spring is as good as standing on the sunny shores of Cancun.

This is why when you see us visiting warmer states such as Florida or California, we wear shorts. Always. Even in the off-season. Even when the natives' limbs are fully covered. We really do know that this makes us stand out, but we don't care. We're not wasting a bit of what qualifies as summer weather in our world. See, we're not crazy. We're hardy. We have a different

Shorts:

Short pants that Minnesotans tend to break out at the first sign of spring.

inner temperature gauge than you do. And you know what? There are people in Minnesota who wear shorts almost straight through the winter. Now *that's* crazy, even by our lax shorts-wearing standards.

Three delicate white petals fan out over its little blushing pouch, or slipper, as the thing's more frequently described. Showy lady's slippers, also called pink-and-white lady's slippers, are a magnificent sight, especially when they reach their maximum height of about 4 feet. They are the state flower, and most Minnesotans could easily pick them out of a lineup of fellow orchids.

It's illegal to pick these lady's slippers, but you can admire them in their natural habitat. They bloom in the northeastern two-thirds of the state in bogs, swamps, roadside ditches, and other cool, damp places between late June and early July. One sure bet is Williams's annual Wildflower Route Celebration. It began in 1990, when then-governor Rudy Perpich declared 81 miles of Highway 11, the main road to Williams, a Minnesota Wildflower Route for the hundreds of thousands of showy lady's slippers that naturally bloom roadside. When the road was expanded about a decade later, many of the flowers were lovingly transplanted. Most made it.

The third Saturday of each June, the folks in Williams map, stake, and identify many wildflowers; chances are good that the state flower will be in bloom then, though it's hard to predict these things. (For more information about this event, call 218–386–2744 or visit www.lakeofthe woodsmn.com/drvwildflower.asp.) You can

Showy Lady's Slipper:

The state flower, found in the swamps, bogs, and ditches of northern and eastern Minnesota. Also known as pink-and-white lady's slipper.

also check with state parks—Lake Bemidji, for example, has a bog walk where showy lady's slippers are easily in view.

Minnesotans consider themselves a hardy people, but we do have our limits. The largest skyway (or elevated walkway) system in the world is proof of this. Minneapolis got its first skyway in 1962. Saint Paul followed suit five years later. Now other cities in Minnesota and beyond have them, too. Each Twin City claims more than 5 miles of skyway, connecting around 100 city blocks. Saint Paul's are uniform, city-built and city-run structures, whereas the various companies behind those in Minneapolis strive for originality with glass roofs, multicolored glass, and metal designs.

Because of the skyways, it sometimes looks as though winter winds and/or snow have driven everyone out of the city. Not so. All the action has just neatly shifted indoors, one story above street level. Once you've ducked into one building, it's probably connected to most of downtown, so you can go to work, shop, drop off your dry cleaning, run to the bank, or hang out at a cafe—all without stepping foot outside. During the lunch hour you see a lot of tennis-shoe-wearing, speed-walking professionals eking out some indoor exercise. It's like a giant Habitrail for humans.

The Minneapolis segments that run over Nicollet Mall really come in handy during the popular Holidazzle Parade, which runs Wednesday through Sunday evenings between Thanksgiving and Christmas each year. Thousands of people bundle up and stand outdoors for this half-hour twinkle-lit evening parade, but the less robust (smarter?) ones stake out skyway spots early for a temperate, bird's-eye view of the sparkly action below.

Skyway:

A system of enclosed glass walkways, connecting the second stories of city buildings, that helps pedestrians avoid winter weather.

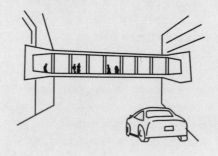

you know you're in
minnesota when...
...you pray for a snow day

A snow day is when schools are closed because of too much snow falling all at once, dangerously low temperatures, and/or icy roads. Naturally, kids root for this. (On the flip side, when Minnesota kids grow to adults they'll be perversely proud if their old schools refuse to shut down, no matter how brutal the blizzard.)

Anyone who grew up in Minnesota can recall waking up to the ground heaped in white, noticing that snow is still falling, then suddenly being hit with the realization that maybe it will be a snow day. There are two benefits to a snow day: no school, and plenty of snow to play with. Faced with the prospect of this double whammy, you run to turn on the TV and plop down in front of it, breathless. A list of schools, followed by each one's verdict, appears on the bottom of the screen. You silently hope against the half day and the measly late start. The jackpot—that's what you're pulling for. When you see your school name followed by "closed," you erupt in a cheer, your excitement level at a height normally reserved for Christmas or your birthday morning.

Yes, an official snow day is like a present. A beautiful, unexpected present. Everything that was supposed to happen has been erased, and all you have before you is one full, clear day, piled with fresh snow.

Snow Day:

A winter day during which the snow is so deep, the temperature is so low, or the roads are so icy that school is called off.

you know you're in
minnesota when...
...snowmobiles race across frozen lakes

When the snow flies in Minnesota, snow-mobilers are suddenly everywhere, especially Up North, where the snow is deepest. They're racing across frozen lakes or down wooded trails or in snow-filled roadside ditches, where there are even little directional and stop signs for them. They're inside road- and lakeside bars and restaurants in boots and thermal bibs, helmets hung on pegs provided for this specific reason, machines parked out front. They're taking pit stops on remote trails to enjoy the view of a stream or Lake Superior or the silent woods, and maybe a swig of schnapps to stay warm.

It only gets cold when you stop, though. Today's high-tech gear plus the heated grips now standard on snowmobiles keep things relatively toasty, not to mention the sweat you work up maneuvering a 500-pound machine through snowy curves at 40 miles an hour.

There are more than 275,000 machines registered in Minnesota. That number, higher than the population of most Minnesota counties, is among the largest in any state. To accommodate these riders, there's a web of more than 20,000 miles of groomed trails (most snowmobile-oriented businesses, such as gas stations, rental shops, and motels, sell maps of their area). Even snowmobilers who have plenty of snow in their own backyard (literally) will trailer their machines to other sections of Minnesota to check out an unfamiliar set of frozen lakes, wooded trails, and snow-filled roadside ditches.

Snowmobiling:

A popular Minnesota pastime that entails driving motorized sleds on trails and across frozen lakes.

Is it any wonder that when SPAM was named, alcohol was involved? On New Year's Eve 1936, in Austin, Minnesota, J. C. Hormel bribed party guests with drinks, one per every name suggested for his company's newest product: canned, spiced ham. It was a slow start for SPAM, but then World War II transformed it from a slightly unsettling concept into a lifesaving one. Durable meat with an incredible shelf life—it made perfect sense to soldiers and citizens alike. And not only Americans. Soviet leader Nikita Khrushchev later wrote, "Without SPAM, we wouldn't have been able to feed our army."

Postwar, SPAM continued to gain international fame that bordered on infamy. Somewhere along the line it transcended its status as a mere meat product to become a cultural icon embraced the world over. To date, more than six billion cans of SPAM have been produced, and the product is trademarked in more than 100 countries on six continents.

Yes, SPAM is everywhere. Especially in its hometown, where light-post banners proudly declare Austin "SPAMtown USA." The 16,500-square-foot SPAM Museum (800–LUV–SPAM, www.spam.com) teaches visitors everything they never knew they wanted to know about the product through videos and interactive games. Admission is free, allowing you to spend all your money in the mammoth gift shop, where there's a SPAM version of practically every household item. Summer's SPAM Museum Jam draws visitors from across the country and around the world for sweet small-town festival events such as a parade and kids' games, plus lots of foods containing SPAM.

Ironically, the nation's other big SPAM festival is in Austin, Texas. It's called SPAMA-RAMA and it's the anti-SPAM Jam, with totally irreverent events such as a SPAM toss and a SPAM-calling contest. Hormel does not sanction SPAMARAMA, presumably because of its undignified nature. They just don't see: SPAM belongs to the people now. You gotta let them show their love any way they know how.

SPAM:

1. Spiced ham in a can. 2. A piece of Americana with its own museum and festival, made by Hormel in Austin, Minnesota.

you know you're in
minnesota when...
...you don't buy something because it's "a little spendy"

In some areas of the country, when people think the price tag on something is too high, they'll call it "costly," "expensive," or "pricey." In Minnesota, it's considered "spendy." Minnesotans in general tend to be, shall we say, thrifty. They're coupon clippers, owners of tip calculators, bulk-food buyers, and finders of out-of-the-way gas stations with prices two cents per gallon cheaper.

Given this fact, "spendy" can be used quite often, and for situations in which a non-Minnesotan wouldn't consider it applicable. Valet parking? Too spendy. Even in the dead of winter, a true Minnesotan would likely self-park and walk. Drive-through car washes? Too spendy, especially when you've got a hose and a bucket at home. (Unless, of course, you've calculated that the money spent on water is more than you'd feed into one of those self-service do-hickeys.)

That said, Minnesotans will splurge. Say, for instance, that you're celebrating your wedding anniversary and your spouse is set on a restaurant with dim lighting, linen napkins, and servers whose outfits do not require a matching hat or visor. In Minnesota you'd likely comment that the place "sounds a little spendy" before agreeing to go. Once at the restaurant, you'd scan the menu for the least spendy entree. If your

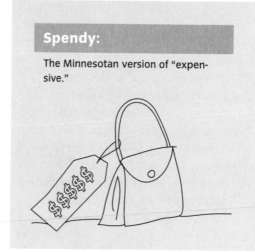

Spendy:

The Minnesotan version of "expensive."

spouse eschewed this rule, you'd say, "Well, you're certainly feeling spendy." If there were leftovers, of course you'd take home a doggie bag. And when others asked how your celebratory meal was, you'd say, "Well, it was good. But it was a little spendy."

you know you're in
minnesota when...
... a giant spoon cradles a water-spewing,
1,200-pound maraschino cherry

The 51-foot-long silver spoon's handle arches over a pond, and its bowl supports a 1,200-pound cherry, misting water from its stem. Designed by Claes Oldenburg and Coosje van Bruggen, a couple world-famous for their oversize depictions of ordinary objects, *Spoonbridge and Cherry* anchors more than 40 permanent sculptures in the 11-acre Minneapolis Sculpture Garden. Depending on where you stand, there are some outstanding views framed by this giant eating utensil, most notably the beautiful Basilica of Saint Mary (the first basilica built in the United States) and the Minneapolis skyline. Lots of wedding parties sprawl on the sculpture garden lawn to incorporate *Spoonbridge and Cherry* and its backdrop into memories of their big day.

The garden is the result of a 1988 collaboration between the Minneapolis Parks and Recreation Board and the Walker Art Center (612–375–7600, www.walkerart.org). It unfolds in front of the Walker, a hip, engaging, internationally respected leader in contemporary arts and in arts education. Founded way back in 1879, the Center's impressive permanent collection of almost 10,000 works includes a huge self-portrait by Chuck Close, a Roy Lichtenstein painting of his studio, and a plaster poodle by Katharina Fritsch. Then there are the political plays, the happy hours, the book club,

the music, the movies. The Walker throws out a lot of intriguing options.

In 2005 the Walker doubled its size with another 130,000 square feet. There's comfortable public space to encourage visitor lounging, plus airy galleries, two Wolfgang Puck–operated restaurants, and an intimate, high-tech theater where visitors can watch performance rehearsals. Once the connected Guthrie Theater moves to its new Minneapolis riverfront location, the sculpture garden will spread out, too, gaining four acres. From the glass walls and rooftop terraces of the Walker, views of the expanded campus—both with and without a giant cherry—will be incredible.

Spoonbridge and Cherry:

The literally named, oversize Oldenburg and van Bruggen sculpture at the Minneapolis Sculpture Garden, in front of the acclaimed Walker Art Center in downtown Minneapolis.

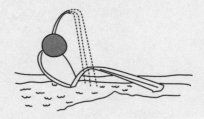

No matter how much pride Minnesotans take in their ability to withstand incredible winters, they're happy to see the first signs of spring. In fact, we'd argue that given the winters we endure, we may be the most spring-appreciative state there is. We are so invigorated by its impending arrival that when the first patch of lawn peeks through the snow, we often pretend that the season is already here. We put on shorts, check tee times, and sometimes even sunbathe. All this before the first bud appears on any tree.

Once there's been a warm enough string of days to banish the final stubborn piles of gray snow, we happily trade storm windows for screens, swap our down jackets for windbreakers, and unearth the gardening tools. As the daffodils, tulips, and lilacs arrive, we pray for a good rain to clean sidewalks and streets of sand, spread for winter traction. Swings and teeter-totters at city parks creak again, and it's hard to find a spot on outdoor patios at restaurants, bars, and cafes. The state really comes to life during these few weeks sandwiched between hot and cold. As the days grow longer, the lakes heat up, and the kids start counting down school days, people wonder aloud when summer will finally arrive.

Spring:

A few weeks somewhere between the end of March and the end of May that are characterized by temperatures consistently above 60, sandy streets, small gray piles of hard snow, and green buds on trees.

Stillwater holds the small-town-tourism tri-fecta: bed-and-breakfasts (more than any other town in the state), antiques stores (the historic downtown is packed with 'em), and a river (the lovely St. Croix). Each of these getaway-draws evokes Stillwater's past, which is also the state's. This *is* the Birthplace of Minnesota.

Among the first settlers here was John McKusick, who set up a sawmill with three other men in 1843. They picked the right spot. The St. Croix could transport logs, and its valley held America's largest stand of white pines. McKusick named the lumber company Stillwater for the Maine town he loved. The St. Croix waters on which he hoped to make a fortune inspired him as well.

Five years later, the company store McKusick built for the sawmill hosted a meeting, the intent of which was to make Minnesota a territory. That happened in 1849—thus Stillwater's Minnesota-birthplace claim. Stillwater boomed as a lumber town through the end of the 19th century.

Many of the lumber barons' opulent Victorian homes are now B&Bs. Mills and other historic buildings house antiques shops, restaurants, and bookstores; downtown is on the National Register of Historic Places. The river, spanned by a pre–World War II vertical lift bridge, is still the town's focal point. People cruise the St. Croix. They kayak it, eat by it, ride hot air balloons over it, and take Venice-style gondola rides on it.

During summer's annual Lumberjack Days, crowds of people float in boats on the river while listening to big-name musicians playing on a riverfront stage. People pack the town for this festival, which features lots of events, including lumberjack exhibitions such as ax throwing, pole climbing, and log rolling. But even when there's not a festival going on, the line of cars heading into town on fair-weather weekends proves that tourism is now the biggest industry in this lumber town where Minnesota was born.

Stillwater:

A popular Minnesota small town known for its lumber-industry roots and its bed-and-breakfasts, antiques shops, and St. Croix River activities.

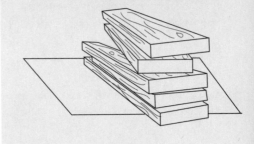

Contrary to the popular belief held by non-Minnesotans, the state does have a season called summer, during which it actually gets hot and muggy enough that we consider central air-conditioning a necessity. In fact, the highest temperature ever recorded in Minnesota was 114 degrees, which beats out the record in both Hawaii and Florida by 14 and 5 degrees, respectively.

The farther north you go, the shorter the season, the cooler the evenings, and the less likely you are to encounter 100-degree-plus temps. But, on average, even the far north will have at least glimpsed the 80s by the end of August.

Minnesotans savor their relatively short summers. This is prime lake-visiting time. Beyond that, we do typical summer things such as head for pools and water parks, linger around ice cream shops, and avoid using the stove. By the end of the season, many of us even start gravitating toward low-lit, air-conditioned homes and businesses and complaining about the hot weather, wondering aloud when fall will finally arrive.

Summer:

Starting sometime in June, about three months of temperatures between 70 and 100 degrees, characterized by sunny, muggy days and warm nights.

Summit Avenue in Saint Paul has always been where the fancy people live. Novelist F. Scott Fitzgerald lived on it for a time, calling his home "a house above average on a street above average." The avenue draws gawkers who marvel at the sprawling, splendid, expensive abodes. One end is marked by the marvelous gold-domed Cathedral of Saint Paul, and the other by the Mississippi River. The avenue runs for 4.5 miles between the two, making it the country's longest and finest stretch of intact residential Victorian housing.

Summit boomed in the 1880s, a time when similar streets were developing in cities across the country, largely out of necessity. Rich people could afford horses, not to mention their care and feeding, and these carriage-pulling symbols of prosperity needed regular exercise on a suitable street. The thing about Summit is that while America's other comparable streets have largely been razed or neglected, Summit has survived mostly intact. About 85 percent of the homes built during its boom remain, and it's now a protected historic district.

Surprisingly, Summit's not all that stuffy, but rather well used, with a nice neighborhoody feel. It's padded by a couple of universities and renovated upper-middle-class neighborhoods, and Grand Avenue, a popular Saint Paul shopping and entertainment

Summit Avenue:

The country's largest stretch of intact, original residential Victorian homes and the fanciest street in Minnesota.

street, is just one block south. Any newer buildings fit, for the most part, with the old rambling homes of varying styles. Some of the older homes are still occupied by single families (like that of the governor); others have been made into condominiums; and still others are owned by a variety of social and cultural organizations. In good weather people walk, run, and bike down the street, and there are usually the aforementioned gawkers.

For a spectacular example of a Victorian home, visit that of railroad baron James J. Hill at 240 Summit, owned and run by the Minnesota Historical Society. The society also gives regular walking tours from May through September—a guided glimpse into the fancy life on Summit Avenue (651–297–2555, www.mnhs.org/visit).

In Minnesota a sweatshirt is not just for working out. In fact, many who wear one on a regular basis never even exercise. This comfy cotton or cotton/polyester article of clothing that resembles a sweater is ubiquitous here. It is practically a state icon, and it represents us well, combining two key characteristics of our people: our casual nature and our inevitable need to stay warm much of the year.

In fall and spring a sweatshirt can be used instead of a jacket. Plenty of people use it the same way in winter, on top of a layer of long underwear. A sweatshirt also comes in handy on chilly summer nights, which are possible anywhere but more common farther north.

Wear the unofficial Minnesota uniform as you will. Although matching pants are certainly not frowned upon, sweatshirts are most often paired with jeans or khakis. Any old sweatshirt will work just fine, but those that have something to do with an upcoming holiday, fishing, or being Norwegian are quite popular, as are those that promote a Minnesota sports team, professional or collegiate. (Go, Gophers!)

The sweatshirt is a practical choice for almost any event in any part of the state. Ladies, do not make the mistake of thinking that sweatshirts are for casual events only. Plenty of them are (or can be) prettied up

with metallic studs, decorative paints, fabric designs, and even buttons up the front. This sort of tricked-out sweatshirt won't get you a second glance in even the fanciest of most Minnesota supper clubs. Unless it's an appreciative glance, that is.

Sweatshirt:

1. A warm article of clothing that resembles a sweater and is smooth on the outside and fuzzy on the inside.
2. The unofficial Minnesota uniform.

you know you're in
minnesota when...
...Target discount store has been in style for decades

Before there were stores in 47 states, before the postmodern advertising campaign, Minnesotans were answering clothing compliments with the hushed, conspiratorial phrase "I got it at Target." This name has been synonymous with a red-and-white bull's-eye for decades here. And we've been ironically pronouncing it with a French accent for just as long, *dahling*. In 1962 the first *Tar-zhay* opened in Roseville, a Saint Paul suburb. Now every Twin Citian knows someone who works for Target.

Fashion-conscious thrifties rejoiced when the Daytons, Minnesota's first family of department stores, trotted out their version of the concept of cool, quality goods at low prices. They only got better at it. By 2000 Target's profit and growth stats were so outstanding that the corporation's name changed from Dayton's to Target. A few years later Target sold the department store that had given birth to it. Now Target is the country's hippest discount chain, where customers spend hours meandering down wide aisles, loading their red shopping carts with ironic T-shirts, funky throw pillows, designer toilet brushes, and actual necessities.

Even way back when, Target made a conscious decision to stay in the city so its employees could be plugged into urban

Target:

A national discount chain developed in Minnesota by department-store icon Dayton's.

trends. In 2001 the company introduced its mark on the Minneapolis skyline: the 34-story Target building topped by an ever-changing band of colored lights. (They even turn it on during dark, dead-of-winter mornings so commuters have something to admire.) Minnesotans see this shimmering skyscraper and think *Target,* just as they, along with the rest of the country, do when they see that ubiquitous red-and-white bull's-eye.

you know you're in
minnesota when...
... sentences regularly end in *then* or *now*

Minnesotans frequently tack *then* or *now* onto the end of sentences. These words may sound extraneous to people from other parts of the country, but in Minnesota they often have a purpose. Admittedly, they are at times used solely to soften a statement, which thereby cultivates the impression of Minnesota Nice. But both words put a slightly different bent on a sentence. Understanding their usage is important if you want to wholly understand, or connect with, a Minnesotan.

Then is the more versatile of the two words. It is commonly used to show agreement, as in, "We'll go ahead with your idea to put butterscotch chips in the bars, then," or the popular "OK, then." Its addition to a sentence can also show, in a polite way, that you'd like to be done with a conversation, as in, "I guess you have that all taken care of, then," or "We'll see you at the lake this weekend, then."

Now does not mean "immediately" in this placement, but it does hint toward urgency, as in, "You take care of that rash, now," or "Don't forget to mow the lawn, now," or the oft-used "Bye, now," which is the preferred phrase to use when leaving the company of a Minnesotan. Especially when coupled with "You drive safe, then."

Until you're comfortable with the *then/now* subtleties, you might want to stick with *then*. It can often replace *now* without causing confusion. As you get more comfortable with these words, play with tone and how it gently shifts meaning. After enough time in Minnesota, you will develop an ear for this.

Then and Now:

Two normally time-oriented words that are regularly tacked onto the ends of sentences in Minnesota.

you know you're in
minnesota when...
...a three-car garage is a standard necessity

There's the boat. The trailer. The snowmobile. The snowblower. Even without taking tools, lawn-care equipment, perhaps a four-wheeler or motorcycle, and actual vehicles into consideration, a measly one- or two-car garage would already be full. For the average Minnesotan who takes full advantage of all four seasons, a three-car garage is not a luxury, it's a necessity. It's not out of the question to see a four- or even five-car garage, or two separate garages on one piece of property—one attached and one detached.

It's common knowledge that any guy with that much stuff in his garage likes to be out there with it. Accordingly, there must be enough space for the necessities that allow him to exist in this grown-man fort of sorts for hours at a time. At the base level these include a heater, a radio, and a refrigerator stocked with enough cans of beer that buddies who swing by unannounced do not have to stand empty-fisted. Other touches: recliners, TVs, phone lines, and a makeshift urinal (a hole cut into the garage wall and fitted with a length of plastic pipe).

All these things create an environment in which it's easier to exist and tinker with all the gadgets and necessities that, for many, enhance the quality of life in Minnesota. So the bigger the garage, the higher the probability that you can fit all your playthings

inside and still have room for the family vehicles. Or maybe one of them. OK, even with more stalls than bedrooms in your house, many family vehicles might have to sit outside.

Three-Car Garage:

A necessity for many Minnesotans who store everything *but* the family car in the garage.

you know you're in
minnesota when...
...the state's longest rivalry lives on

Though their downtowns are just 11 miles apart and their metro areas blend together seamlessly, you cannot confuse one Twin City for the other. For one thing, their residents won't let you. A Minneapolite might call Saint Paul boring and old-fashioned next to his own hip, exciting town. And a Saint Paulite would say her city is classic and down-to-earth, not like snooty, trend-chasing Minneapolis. Ah, sibling rivalry.

This bickering was born with the cities. Saint Paul started on the east bank, at the highest navigable point in the Mississippi. Minneapolis sprouted on the west bank, at the power source of St. Anthony Falls. Both boomed because of the waterway, but each was jealous of what it gave the other. Saint Paul earned the title of territory, then state capital, and grabbed other victories, such as the permanent site of the state fair. Minneapolis had its own string of wins, including the airport, the university, and all the big sports teams.

One of the most storied examples of the cities at war is the census of 1890. When the tallies showed that Minneapolis's population had significantly surpassed Saint Paul's, the capital city cried fraud. Initial investigations showed both real and non-existent Minneapolis homes packed with imaginary residents. Minneapolis launched its own attack, and Saint Paul was none the

Twin Cities' Rivalry:

A longstanding competition between Minneapolis and Saint Paul, the state's two largest cities, which reside on opposite banks of the Mississippi River.

purer. After recounts Minneapolis was still bigger. It has remained so ever since.

Now Minneapolis sits at about 383,000 residents, Saint Paul has roughly 96,000 fewer, and the rivalry still exists. It probably always will. Deep down, we know that each city has its good qualities, even if stubborn pride won't always let that be voiced. On the bright side, stubborn pride is still pride, which probably wouldn't exist in such a strong form without this longstanding rivalry.

you know you're in
minnesota when...
...you hear someone utter "Uff da"

Uff da is a Norwegian exclamation of surprise, annoyance, commiseration, or displeasure. Insert *uff da* where you might normally use any of the following phrases or their synonyms: oops, ouch, oh my, wow, *oy vey,* and good grief.

One beauty of *uff da* is that it's onomatopoeic (for those of you who are not word geeks, this means that it sounds like its meaning). If it sounds, or more importantly *feels,* as though it might fit, it probably does. It's just that easy. Which is probably the reason that it's the only surviving, universally used Norwegian phrase in a state riddled with descendants of Norwegians—America's largest population of them, in fact. Here are some situations in which one might use the phrase *uff da*:

- when you're moving something heavy
- when you discover that the dog has peed on the carpet
- when the supper tab turns up much higher than you'd expected
- when you step outside of your temperate home to weather that's really cold or really hot
- when someone tells you that they arrived late because of a mildly unfortunate incident, such as a parking ticket or road construction.

Uff Da:

A Scandinavian-based exclamation of surprise, annoyance, or exertion.

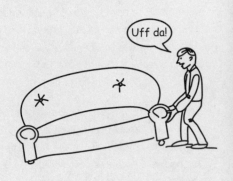

You get the idea. For the record, it's very much acceptable for people not of Scandinavian descent to use *uff da*. If it feels a bit unnatural at first, you're welcome to warm up by using the shortened version, *uff*.

Every Minnesotan goes Up North. This is the shortened version of "to a cabin, a second home, or any kind of lodging that's north of where I currently am." Generally, Up North is at least an hour north of the Twin Cities, where the treeline begins. But people living farther north, such as in Brainerd, think you have to drive farther still to truly be Up North.

Any Up North location is likely on or near a lake. Although a body of water is often the reason for going Up North, even if simply to provide a nice view during a winter weekend getaway, this is not always the case. One might go Up North simply to take long hikes in the woods or to hunt, for example.

Take note that people south of Minnesota, such as Iowans, call our entire state "Up North." Though that may be true for them, this definition doesn't fly in Minnesota. When here, stick to the strictest definition of the term if you care to be taken seriously.

It's important to note that Up North is not necessarily interchangeable with going to "the lake." You may be going to the lake when going Up North, but this is not guaranteed. Conversely, you could go to the lake and not be Up North. Don't feel bad if this is difficult to understand. It is a fine distinction easily discernible only to Minnesota natives and long-timers—and it's a good bet that even among them, there would be disagreement as to the correct definition.

Up North:

A cabin, a second home, or any kind of lodging in Minnesota that's north of where you are when you use the term.

you know you're in
minnesota when...
...you're houseboating in Voyageurs National Park

Two centuries ago, French-Canadian canoemen called *voyageurs* paddled 35-foot birch-bark boats from Lake Superior to Lake of the Woods, using the water highway through a chain of lakes to exchange furs for trade goods. That highway of sorts became the boundary of Minnesota and Canada, and now 55 miles of it is also the border of Voyageurs, Minnesota's only national park. (Just southeast of the park is the Boundary Waters Canoe Area Wilderness, a similar tract of land that, unlike Voyageurs, does not allow motors.) The park's 218,200 acres are more than one-third water, and the only way to access the bulk of the park is by boat or float plane.

After the voyageurs came gold miners, loggers, and commercial fishermen. Before them came the Native Americans, as well as four rounds of glaciers that crept in and barreled out of this area, creating more than 30 pristine lakes loaded with hundreds of rocky, pine-covered islands and lots of barrier reefs. Tourism has been the only industry since the establishment of the park in 1975. Although navigating the lakes can be challenging, it's well worth the park's stunning, unspoiled views and world-famous fishing for walleye, northern pike, smallmouth bass, and even the elusive muskie.

Houseboats are a popular and comfortable way to experience the park, and its massive acreage means that secluded inlets are plentiful. Most people still stop by the park's big man-made attraction, historic Kettle Falls Hotel, where lumberjacks once slept. It has a restaurant as well as a bar; in the latter the floor slopes so steeply that one side of the pool table is built up an extra 18 inches. When the floor starts to look level, it's time to go to bed.

Voyageurs National Park:

1. Minnesota's only national park. 2. A 218,200-acre water-based park comprising 134,000 land acres, most of which are accessible only by boat or float plane.

you know you're in
minnesota when...
...you're eating walleye, the state fish

Yes, these fish are also named walleyed pike, but don't call them that when you're in Minnesota. Just call them walleye. They're found in many of the state's lakes, and good-size walleye are a prized, though absolutely attainable, catch. Even big walleye are usually gentle on the fishing line, and they clean up well—not a lot of bones. Their meat is white and flaky and best served battered and deep-fried, with tartar sauce and lemon, alone or on a bun. (Health nuts, go ahead and eat them broiled, but you're missing out.) Diners, supper clubs, and bars across the state serve this treat on the regular menu as well as during ever-popular Friday fish-frys.

A number of walleye sites and festivals around Minnesota pay tribute to the state's beloved and tasty swimmer. The communities of Isle, Rush City, Garrison, Baudette, and Ray all have giant walleye statues that are fun to pose in front of. (Since the one in Ray inexplicably wears a saddle, you can pretend to ride it, too.) Both Garrison and Baudette bill themselves as the Walleye Capital of the World. Baudette's fiberglass fish is bigger—40 feet versus Garrison's measly 15. But Garrison's sits along 200-square-mile Lake Mille Lacs, one of the state's premier walleye lakes. You be the judge.

Walleye:

1. A North American freshwater sport fish with prominent eyes. 2. The Minnesota state fish.

Even though Laura Ingalls Wilder lived in several Midwestern states during her nomadic late-1800s pioneer life, she's indelibly linked chiefly to Walnut Grove, Minnesota. Her books tell of the family's four years in town, broken up by a one-year stint in Iowa, but writers for the 1970s TV series chose to let things unfold neatly in Walnut Grove. They called the series *Little House on the Prairie,* the title of Wilder's second book, which, incidentally, took place in Kansas.

In the TV show, basically anything that took place in Laura's life and books took place in Walnut Grove, along with plenty of things that never happened at all. (Sometimes even prairie life is not dramatic enough for TV.) It's safe to say that by the ninth season—which featured an orangutan, a drugged sideshow attraction named Wild Boy, and a well accident in which a down-and-out dwarf saves the day—things had significantly strayed from little Half Pint's original prairie experience. That was the show's last season. In its final episode the townspeople blew up Walnut Grove.

Walnut Grove holds no grudges. Each year the town stages a Wilder Pageant, an outdoor drama that stays truer to the real story of the Ingalls family, along the banks of Plum Creek. It's a highlight of the July Family Festival, which also features a Laura

Walnut Grove:

A town in Minnesota made famous by the book and TV show *Little House on the Prairie*.

and Nellie look-alike contest, in which girls ages 8 through 12 are judged based on their knowledge of and resemblance to the two *Little House* characters. Visitors also can check out a depression in the earth where the family's sod house once stood; it's on a farm whose owners charge a small fee. In town, the Laura Ingalls Wilder Museum has some late-1800s buildings as well as artifacts relating to the real Ingalls family and its TV-star counterparts. And just east of Walnut Grove in the town of Sanborn, the Sod House on the Prairie bed-and-breakfast lets you spend a night Ingalls-style, prairiewear and all.

Because of its extreme and ever-changing nature in Minnesota, weather is a popular conversation starter with friends and family as well as acquaintances and strangers. Some standard phrases are, "Cold/hot enough for you?" and "Well, you couldn't ask for a better day," and "They say we'll get another 5 inches before this thing stops."

While observations and information are welcome, complaints are not. The overall tone should be one of camaraderie. A complaint would give the impression that you expected the listener to feel sorry for you, which he or she most certainly won't. Unacceptable: "Four feet of snow in one day is ridiculous. I was freezing the entire time I was out there shoveling, and my back hurts now." Acceptable: "She's sure coming down. Took me two hours to clear the driveway." The listener will assume, from experience, that it was a cold two hours and that your back hurts. If he or she feels like continuing the conversation, it will likely involve an inquiry into the state of your back or a statement that plays off what you said, such as, "Yeah, me too."

It's also common to pull out past weather events to illustrate that it's been either better or (usually) worse than what you're experiencing now. Don't be surprised if someone says, "You think a foot is something? During the Armistice Day Blizzard of

1940, I couldn't see the roof of the garage." Speculation is popular, too, as in, "What kind of winter do you think we'll get?" We're curious about what's around the bend, but we know enough not to assume anything. Weather has taught Minnesotans that things could always get better and they could always get worse, but one thing's for sure: They'll change.

Weather:

A popular conversation topic among both friends and strangers in Minnesota.

you know you're in
minnesota when...
... wild rice really is wild

Don't be fooled by the name *wild rice.* Some of it is not, in fact, wild. For the past 50 years or so, farmers in Minnesota and beyond have cultivated it in paddies. Given that *wild* is in the grain's name, this can be tricky.

If you define *wild rice* in the strictest of terms—meaning that you count only that which develops when nature does its thing—Minnesota is the world leader in its production. It's our state grain, a category that was likely invented to honor its natural abundance here. We grow a lot of "wild" wild rice.

It makes sense, then, that the hearty brown grain is sold in tourist shops and offered in restaurants, usually as a side dish or in soup, to which it adds a great nutty flavor. You'll find it mostly in the central and northern parts of the state, where it grows abundantly. There, Native Americans who have relied on wild rice for hundreds of years still harvest it on reservations the old-fashioned way. One person pushes a canoe with a forked pole while another gently beats the grassy stems, knocking rice into the canoe. Whatever doesn't make it into the canoe serves as food for waterfowl or seed for next year's crop of wild rice—by the strictest definition, of course.

Wild Rice:

1. A common ingredient in soups and side dishes, especially in central and northern Minnesota. 2. The state grain.

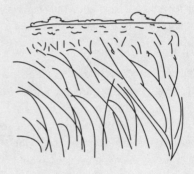

Winter is Minnesota's most storied season, and deservedly so. It's our longest—as long as the other three combined—and it usually gets really snowy and unbelievably cold. Below-zero days are commonplace. In fact, there are times when the temperature everywhere in the state starts with a minus sign. When it's exceedingly cold in other parts of America, national newscasts report the temperature in International Falls, Minnesota, as a reminder that things could be worse.

Even though it looks impressively low, forget the temperature. It's an irrelevant number that tells how cold it is in—how's this for a useless phrase?—"ideal conditions." Pay attention, instead, to the wind chill, which takes wind speed into account to tell you how cold it "feels" outside. Everyone except the meteorologist will tell you that how cold it *feels* outside is how cold it *is* outside.

That said, you can't tell the difference between -20 and -30 anyway. It's cold here. Always has been. So buck up. You can do practically everything in winter that you do at any other time of year; the human body, if dressed appropriately, is remarkably adaptive. Go sledding or snowmobiling or skiing or something. Even just go for a walk. Life does not stop for the snow or the cold here—Minnesotans are more likely to feel sorry for themselves in the dog days of summer than in the dead of winter.

Granted, once April hits and the snow is still here and the days get longer, people start getting antsy, and they begin to wonder aloud when spring will finally arrive.

Winter:

A snowy, cold time of year—starting as early as October and ending as late as May—during which temperatures can drop well below zero.

you know you're in
minnesota when...
...sentences regularly end in *with*

In Minnesota it is perfectly acceptable to end sentences with the word *with*. Example: "We're going to see the new art exhibit at the Walker. Would you like to come with?"

This is proper usage here, despite what is taught in schools. It's our little footnote to the rules of grammar (one that exists only within the state's boundaries), a quirky departure from the norm—kind of like how Arizona refuses to play along with Daylight Saving Time or Michigan requires drivers to participate in an intricate system of detours in order to complete a left-hand turn. Ending a sentence with *with* is our thing.

Seriously—we do not want to hear about dangling prepositions. There's no need to get uppity. It's not as if you don't know what we're talking about. When someone says, "Hey, I got an extra ticket to the Gopher game on Sunday. Wanna come with?" you know darn well what that means. You don't need the word *me* there at the end. That's practically long-winded.

We're a people of few words. In fact, we're a bit suspicious of anyone who seems to take pride in the sound of his or her own voice. And of anyone who insists that, even in the state of Minnesota, you can't end a sentence with *with*. An uninvited

grammar lesson won't get you far here. More importantly, it certainly won't get you that extra ticket to the game.

With:

A preposition that Minnesotans often purposefully leave dangling.

Want to come with?

It's true. Even though the movie _Fargo_ blew our accent and verbal tics out of proportion for comedic effect, Minnesotans do use the phrase _you betcha_. This is an affirmative response along the lines of _yes, OK,_ or _sure_. For example, suppose that your neighbor said, "I was thinkin' that we'd have a little potluck picnic now that the weather's nice. Sound good?" or "You headed to The Cities again this year to do some school shopping?" The appropriate positive response in both cases would be "You betcha."

_Ya_, a form of _yes_, often precedes _you betcha_. This is solely the speaker's preference and does not necessarily reflect an enhanced state of agreement. Meaning that if you answered the example questions above with "Ya, you betcha," you would not automatically imply that you were really excited about the potluck picnic or especially enthusiastic about your annual school-shopping trip to The Cities. Such feeling is shown solely through tone. A flat tone connotes plain-old agreement, whereas an animated tone infers excitement.

Ya, you betcha can be personalized. Experiment with drawing the _ya_ out. ("Yaaaah.") Substitute _you bet_ for _you betcha_. Or drop the _you betcha_ altogether and just use _ya_.

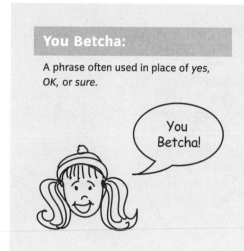

You Betcha:

A phrase often used in place of _yes, OK,_ or _sure_.

Mix and match these styles of agreement to find the one that best suits particular situations or your personal preferences.

index